EXPECTATIONS

How Teacher Expectations Can Increase Student Achievement and Assist in Closing the Achievement Gap

Section I
The Research on Teacher Expectations

Section II
**What Effective Teachers Do:
Best Practices**

Robert L. Green, Ph.D.

Columbus, OH

The **McGraw·Hill** Companies

Robert L. Green is dean and professor emeritus of urban affairs at Michigan State University, East Lansing, Michigan. This publication is an outgrowth of the author's research and practice in both universities and urban school systems, including Michigan State University; the University of the District of Columbia; the Portland, Oregon, school district; Memphis, Tennessee, City Schools; the Detroit Public Schools; the Dallas Independent School District; the San Francisco Unified School District; and the Piney Woods School, Piney Woods, Mississippi. He is still very involved in an assessment and monitoring role in selected school districts nationally.

SRAonline.com

Send all inquiries to:
SRA/McGraw-Hill
8787 Orion Place
Columbus, OH 43240-4027

Printed in the United States of America.

ISBN 0-07-603662-6

1 2 3 4 5 6 7 8 9 DBH 12 11 10 09 08 07 06 05 04

The McGraw·Hill Companies

ACKNOWLEDGEMENTS

Special thanks go to Bradley Carl, Ph.D. candidate in sociology at Michigan State University, for his research assistance in the preparation of aspects of this document and to Eugenia Zerbinos, Ph.D., for editing and research assistance.

Thanks also go to my wife Lettie and my sons Robert Vincent Green, Kurt Green and Kevin Green for their never-ending support of my work and their assistance in helping to shape my thinking on urban education and holding high expectations for student achievement. My son Kevin, who has a Ph.D. in engineering, has been particularly focused on holding high expectations for minority youngsters in the math and science areas.

Also helping to shape my thinking about urban issues has been my research team that includes Dr. Robert J. Griffore, Dr. John H. Schweitzer, Dr. Lillian Phenice, Dr. Ron Hall, Dr. Eugenia Zerbinos, several graduate students, former urban superintendents Matthew Prophet of Portland, Oregon, Art Jefferson of Detroit, and the Honorable Willie Herenton of Memphis, who focused on the politics of education and student achievement, the late Ron Edmonds, founder of the Effective Schools Movement, and finally to my parents, Thomas and Alberta Green, who always believed in the power of education and high expectations.

TABLE OF CONTENTS

Section I

Section II

EXPECTATIONS

How Teacher Expectations Can Increase
Student Achievement and Assist in
Closing the Achievement Gap

Section I

The Research
on Teacher Expectations

Introduction—The Achievement Gap

Education is perhaps the most powerful force in America related to improving one's status in life. It is widely accepted, in fact, that education is the single most important factor in improving one's socioeconomic status. This may be especially true for racial minorities and others of low socioeconomic status who have not shared equally in the rewards of America's economic prosperity. Education offers a way to break down barriers such as poverty and racial injustice by opening doors to better employment opportunities and political empowerment. In addition to its significance for individuals, educational success is also important for neighborhoods, states, and the nation as a whole in the form of increased earnings and contributions to society. As Fischer *et al.* (1996) and others have noted, a symbiotic relationship between education and prosperity exists, both on an individual and a societal level:

> The amount of schooling young Americans receive heavily determines the jobs they get and the income they make. In turn, educational policies—what sorts of schools are provided, the way school resources are distributed (usually according to the community in which children live), teaching methods such as tracking, and so on—strongly affect how much school[ing] children receive. Similarly, local employment opportunities constrain how well people can do economically (Fischer *et al.*, 1996, p. 9).

Data published by the National Center for Education Statistics confirm the economic significance of education. In 2000, the median annual earnings (in constant 2000 dollars) of adult males ages 25-34 who had a bachelor's degree or higher were $42,292. This was nearly $16,000 higher than the median earnings of those with a high school diploma or GED ($26,399) and more than $23,000 higher than those with less than a high school education ($19,255). Among females of the same age group, median earnings in 2000 for those with a bachelor's degree ($32,238) were nearly twice as high as for high school graduates/GED recipients ($16,573) and almost three times as high as for those with less than a high school education ($11,583). Furthermore, the data confirm that the earning power of those with a high school education or less has declined substantially over the past three decades with the loss of formerly abundant high-paying, low skill manufacturing jobs. In 1971, a male worker age 25-34 with less than a high school education earned a median income (again in constant 2000 dollars) of $31,039, but earned only $19,255 in 2000 (National Center for Education Statistics, 2002).

Despite widespread acknowledgement that education plays a key role in determining future economic success, student achievement data continue to show quite clearly that academic performance and attainment—and thus the economic rewards they confer—are distributed very unevenly. Recent research confirms that the performance of many poor and non-white students, particularly those in urban areas, lags far behind that of their more affluent and white peers. For example, data from the 2002 administration of the National Assessment of Educational Progress (NAEP, often referred to as the "nation's report card") show that among 4th graders in reading (see Figure 1), the average scaled scores of white (228) and Asian American (226) students were substantially higher than for blacks (200) and Hispanics (201). Among 8th grade students, the reading scores of white (272) and Asian (268) students again exceed those of blacks (245) and Hispanics (246). Among 12th graders, reading scores for white (292) and Asian (285) students were again higher than for black (266) and Hispanic (270) students. It should be noted that these trends are largely unchanged since 1992, when the first NAEP data were published (National Center for Education Statistics, 2003).

Figure 1: 2002 NAEP Reading Performance for Grades 4, 8, and 12

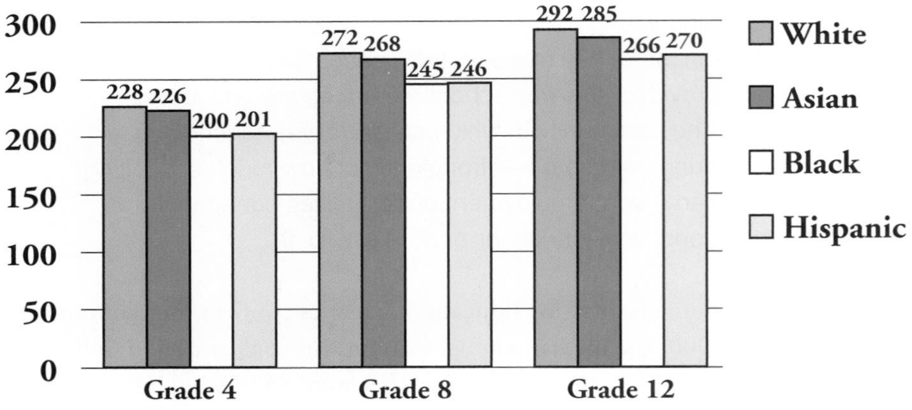

Source: National Center for Education Statistics, 2003.

Figure 2 shows math data from 2000, and the trends are largely the same. White 4th graders (average scaled score 235) again scored much higher than their black (205) and Hispanic (211) peers. Among 8th grade students, both white (285) and Asian (288) students outperformed blacks and Hispanics by at least 33 points. For 12th graders, the gaps are even more evident: scores of 307 and 318 for whites and Asians, respectively, compared to 273 for blacks and 281 for Hispanics (National Center for Education Statistics, 2003).

Figure 2: 2000 NAEP Math Performance for Grades 4, 8, and 12

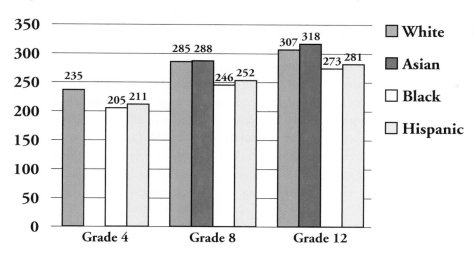

Note: Grade 4 math data contained an insufficient number of Asian students to be included in the final NAEP analyses.

Source: National Center for Education Statistics, 2003.

NAEP data also show very clearly the effects of poverty and living in an urban environment upon performance, regardless of race. Fourth grade results in reading from 2002, for example, show that students eligible for free and reduced price school lunches (average scaled scores of 202) score much lower than do those who are not eligible (229). Similarly, students who attend school in central city locations (average scaled score 208) perform at lower levels than do their urban fringe (221) and rural (219) counterparts (National Center for Education Statistics, 2003).

Recent research by Haycock (2001) shows that achievement gaps that exist at the elementary, middle, and high school levels translate quite clearly into disparities in educational attainment—which in turn fuel disparities in income discussed previously. Among 18-24 year olds, for example, about 90% of whites and 94% of Asians have either completed high school or earned a GED, compared to 81% for African Americans and 63% for Latinos. Perhaps even more telling, African Americans and Latinos are approximately one-half and one-third as likely, respectively, than whites to earn a bachelor's degree.

As the statistics above illustrate, the challenge of providing a quality education to all students is perhaps especially difficult in the schools of our nation's major cities, where many of the most pervasive problems of our society are most evident. Some of these problems—such as high rates of poverty, unemployment, family instability, violence, crime, and drug abuse— are readily measured and are of daily concern to policymakers and educators alike. Related issues such as a sense of despair and hopelessness, along with difficulty understanding the link between education and success, are less conducive to measurement, but represent significant obstacles to the success of urban students (see, for example, Jencks, 1992; Jencks & Peterson, 1991; Jencks & Phillips, 1998; Kotlowitz, 1991; Kozol, 1968, 1991; Anyon, 1997: MacLeod, 1995).

During the 1960s, many educational experts took the position that schools were helpless to teach students living in environments controlled by poverty, broken homes, and crime. In fact, nearly a half century ago a landmark study mandated by Congress, *Equality of Educational Opportunity*, concluded that ". . . Taking all results together, one implication stands out above all: That schools bring little influence to bear on a child's achievement that is independent of his background and general social context" (Coleman *et al.*, 1966, p. 325). It is less likely to hear such overt skepticism about schools nowadays, the same type of thinking has clearly been present in the acceptance of low student performance on the part of urban teachers and administrators, and excuses such as poverty that are offered in explanation of this destructive trend. Poverty is not a barrier to learning, but low expectations, rejection, and indifference are.

Fortunately, educational researchers and practitioners since the 1960s have taken a very different view in concluding that poverty and other social maladies need not doom children to chronically low levels of achievement. The founder of the Effective Schools Movement, Ron Edmonds, maintained that poverty need not be a barrier to educational success, and that all children can learn. Edmonds' work at Harvard and Michigan State University, as well as his experience in the New York Public Schools, supported the position that when the principles of effective schooling—as discussed in more detail below—are in place, young people make strong educational progress regardless of social and economic barriers (see Edmonds, 1979; see also Rutter & Maughan, 2002; Morrison & Connor, 2002; Hughes, 2002; Evans, 2002; Johnson *et al.*, 2000; Brookover, 1977; Brookover *et al.*, 1979; Green, 1977, 1996, 1998, 2003).

It is also fortunate that there exist today a host of urban districts and schools offering proof that poverty and other socioeconomic factors need not serve as a barrier to high academic achievement. Several major urban districts with which I have worked offer examples in which a commitment to improved performance has brought tangible results in terms of higher test scores, reduced dropout rates, and a general sense of enthusiasm and optimism that had long been lacking. In Dallas, for example, African American students had composite gains (as measured by the percentage of those scoring at the satisfactory level or above) of 30.7 points in reading and 46.0 points in math between 1994 and 2002; for Hispanics, the gains were 21.1 points in reading and 39.4 in math. These gains have occurred despite the presence of substantial poverty and language proficiency issues, with nearly three-fourths (74.4%) of Dallas students classified as economically disadvantaged and 29% receiving bilingual/English as a Second Language (ESL) services. Achievement gaps between African American and Hispanic students in Dallas and their white peers have also decreased considerably with the white vs. African American gap shrinking by 17.8 points in reading between 1994 and 2002 and 20.7 points in math. The white vs. Hispanic gap shrank 8.2 points in reading and 14.1 in math. High school completion rates for African Americans in Dallas are higher than for whites in the district (and higher than for African American students in Texas as a whole), and completion rates for Hispanics have also risen steadily over the past four years. Eight of every ten African American students in Dallas graduates in four years, as do nearly three-fourths (72.8%) of Hispanics (see Green, 2002).

Dallas is not the only urban success story. Charlotte-Mecklenburg, North Carolina, which was one of ten large urban districts that volunteered to set a new "urban benchmark" for the NAEP, was the only district where students met the national average in reading and exceeded it in math (Council of the Great City Schools, 2003a, 2003b; Feller, 2003). In response to the release of statistics from Charlotte and other urban centers, Darvin Winick, chairman of the independent board that oversees the NAEP, stated that ". . . [the results] just remove . . . one of the excuses: 'We can't educate them because they're in the inner city.'" Modest progress has also been made in raising test scores in the Detroit Public Schools. Having worked with this district for the past several years, I have also seen a boost in teacher morale and expectations, along with general, research based perceptions that the district is headed in the right direction (see Green, 2003).

Few educators or policymakers in Dallas or in other urban areas where improvement has occurred would claim that the job of having all children achieve at high levels is anywhere near finished, but few would disagree that much-needed progress is being made. Dallas Superintendent Mike Moses echoed the feeling of teachers, administrators, and community members that the challenge is not over. Such progress has become necessary not just because of the importance of education in economic development, but because efforts to improve achievement and address persistent gaps in student achievement along racial and socioeconomic lines have become a major educational priority for the federal government, states, and local school districts. The most notable of these initiatives is the recent No Child Left Behind Act of 2002, which has introduced at the federal level a new age of accountability in which schools are required to test all of their students and to report scores by subgroups in accordance with race/ethnicity and socioeconomic and disability status (see Education Week on the Web, 2004; Robelen, 2004). A series of sanctions and assistance, ranging from additional teacher training to permitting parents to remove their children from schools that fail to demonstrate adequate improvement, are at the heart of this important and controversial new legislation, which may prove to have important ramifications for urban schools. It is important to note that No Child Left Behind has been accompanied by a host of initiatives undertaken at the state and local levels in which policymakers and school administrators are devoting additional time and resources toward addressing low achievement and achievement gaps.

MAJOR CHARACTERISTICS OF EFFECTIVE SCHOOLS: A BRIEF SUMMARY

How have urban districts gone about the monumental task of improving achievement for their students and closing achievement gaps? No single strategy has proven to be the "magic bullet" that is effective immediately, across the board, and at low cost. Rather, a multi-faceted set of approaches has proven most successful, with an appropriate mix of research-validated strategies and flexibility at the district and school level. Research on effective schools has recognized that the specific factors necessary for success in a given district or school may vary somewhat. The literature on effective schools provides a wealth of detail regarding a set of core principles that are associated with high-performing schools (see, for example, Edmonds, 1979; Evans, 2002; Morrison & Connor, 2002; Johnson *et al.*, 2000; Brookover & Lezotte, 1977; Network for Effective Schools, 1987; Benjamin, 1979; Fiske, 1992; Robinson, 1985; Redding, 1997; Walberg, 1984; Wang *et al.*, 1994). It is possible to present a summary description of this body of information under seven general categories. My personal observations in numerous successful urban classrooms during the past decade have noted that these research-based principles are being used. The first six are briefly described below, whereas the seventh, *High Expectations for Student and Teacher Performance*, is the primary subject of this paper.

EFFECTIVE LEADERSHIP

Research has confirmed that effective schools have effective leadership, indicating that the principal is the significant person promoting school-wide improvement (Cotton, 2003). Recognizing this, the Detroit Public Schools, under the leadership of CEO Dr. Kenneth Burnley, instituted a Principals Academy to focus on principal leadership and developing a teacher skill set. Effective principals tend to be highly task-oriented, can clearly articulate the mission of their schools, and expect their staff to follow their leadership. Curricula are carefully coordinated, and high standards are maintained for teacher performance. Effective principals also place a high value on instructional time spent on task, with minimal interruptions of the teaching process. They are also skilled at managing staff conflict and maintaining good relationships with school boards, government officials, and business and civic interests (McEvoy, 2003; Fullan, 2002; Uchiyama & Wolf, 2002; Ubben *et al.*, 2001; Tucker & Codding, 1998; Hirsch, 1996; Hallinger & Murphy, 1986; Grant, 1985; Bunzel, 1985; Squires, Huitt, & Segars, 1983).

ORDERLY ENVIRONMENT

The orderly environment of effective schools is also shown to be an important element in their success. Described in idealized terms as a "business-like atmosphere" (Lezotte, 1980) or possessing a positive ethos (Grant, 1985), this environment is safe, structured, functional, and comfortable. Within such a setting, students and school staff are able to concentrate on the jobs at hand (i.e., teaching and learning) rather than on immediate anxieties and distracting events. One important form this has taken is through class size reduction, particularly in grades K-3, and in schools with large numbers of children who have experienced low levels of academic success. Although research on the long-term effects of class size reduction has been somewhat mixed, it has generally shown that such initiatives have a measurable payoff for low-income and minority students where they have been implemented (see Smith *et al.*, 2003; Finn, 2002; Biddle & Berliner, 2002; McCafferty, 1998). Class size reduction efforts, which typically involve additional resources to limit class sizes to no more than 20 (and in some cases no more than 15), have proven to be strongly supported by teachers and parents where enacted (Mayes, 1998; McCafferty, 1998), although some concerns have arisen about the need to hire additional (and perhaps unqualified) teachers and to construct additional facilities in difficult budgetary times to accommodate these efforts (see Sack, 1999). Other strategies for establishing orderly schools have included reducing school violence by declaring "safe zones" around schools (see Conway & Verdugo, 1999), conducting weapons searches, and requiring the use of uniforms by students to eliminate competition and unrest associated with clothing (see Hoge *et al.*, 2002; White, 2000). An orderly environment must be a priority for effective principals.

ASSESSMENT OF STUDENT PERFORMANCE AND FEEDBACK

Regular assessment of student performance is another recognized component of effective schools when accompanied by timely feedback to students and teachers regarding performance. Administrators and staff within effective schools use assessments, frequently tied to state-defined standards and measured through state-sanctioned standardized tests such as the Michigan Educational Assessment Program (MEAP), to measure their progress and to identify areas in need of improvement. As indicated in the discussion of the No Child Left Behind legislation, assessments have become an increasingly important—and controversial—form of measuring the performance of students and staff, particularly given that a growing number of states and school districts have created "high stakes" tests by linking performance of students to promotion and even teacher pay. Effective schools meet the challenge of assessments head on and use them as a way to improve student achievement rather than attempting to make excuses for poor performance. Standardized tests, of course, need not—and should not—be the only means through which effective schools assess their performance. A more well-rounded set of measures including monitoring of attendance and behavior, retention rates, and qualitative (as opposed to strictly quantitative) evaluation of student work should be the goal of teachers within these schools are clear about their goals and aware of their progress (see Solomon, 2002; Sloane & Kelly, 2003; Haycock, 2002; Tucker & Codding, 1998; Hirsch, 1996).

TIME SPENT DIRECTLY AND EFFICIENTLY ON TEACHING ESSENTIAL ACADEMIC SKILLS

Within the classrooms of effective schools, high levels of student achievement are a direct result of time spent directly on the task at hand, and on the clear and efficient transmission of knowledge from teacher to student. Devotion of maximum time to building basic academic skills and spending maximum time on task can be significantly aided by community involvement. An effective classroom has clearly identified learning objectives (organized by subject as well as by year, month, week, and day), minimized classroom disruptions, and maximized spending more time on task to ensure that teachers, through staff development, know the importance of staying on task. All learning-related activities, from classroom lessons to homework and out-of-school activities such as field trips, should be organized around and aligned with clearly-defined academic objectives. An emphasis on reading, writing, and mathematics is the cornerstone of systematic plans to achieve student proficiency in basic skill areas and to ameliorate learning difficulties experienced by students, and it is these subject areas that tend to be emphasized most in state assessments. An emphasis on basic skills has become particularly important given the increasingly technology-driven nature of the job market, as a solid foundation in reading, writing, and math is a prerequisite for more advanced study in fields such as computers and engineering (see Darling-Hammond & Youngs, 2002; Darling-Hammond, 2001; Danielson, 2001; Sizer, 1984, 1992, 1996; Comer, 1995, 1996, 1997; Rigsby, Stull, Morse-Kelley, 1997; Benjamin, 1979; and Pressley, *et al.*, 2003).

HIGH QUALITY STAFF DEVELOPMENT

Research on effective schools and student achievement is unanimous in concluding that high quality staff development activities are a critical determinant of success. Harvard University scholar Ronald Ferguson (1998), in fact, found that high quality teaching was even more important than family income as a determinant of student achievement, with quality of teaching (as measured by test scores on teacher certification exams, possession of master's degrees, and years of experience) accounting for as much as 43% of the difference in student achievement (Ferguson, 1998). As noted elsewhere in this document, 63 percent of Detroit Public School teachers have a master's degree or higher. In addition, extensive staff development in the Detroit Public Schools has led to improvement in reading in that district. Staff development in Detroit and in the Dallas Independent School District is related to strengthening the core curriculum in reading and math. Professional development activities have long been a part of what teachers do, and are required to do, but recent research and additional attention on the part of the federal government, states, and school districts has identified particularly effective components of successful professional development activities. In brief, high quality professional development activities are ongoing (as opposed to "one shot" activities with no follow-up), regular (as opposed to infrequent), and highly relevant to teachers (see Desimone *et al.*, 2003; Porter *et al.*, 2003). Teachers are given training in effective strategies, the application of research findings, and the principles and practices of effective schools in general.

As I have noted in earlier work (see Green, 1985), in order to be successful, effective professional development programs need to commit adequate time and resources to the task at hand, and must not seek "quick fix" and/or low cost solutions—a task made more difficult by recent budgetary constraints faced by many school districts. Staff development programs must also be subjected to regular evaluation and revision, with the goal of being responsive to the needs of specific school communities. A particular challenge in this respect faces urban schools, whose students and barriers to learning might not be adequately addressed by traditional professional development activities. Fortunately, research on effective professional development activities tailored specifically to urban settings is emerging (see Phillips, 2003; Rashid, 2000; Fermanich, 2002). My own work in urban districts around the country (see Green, 1985, 2002) has shown that staff development is important to improving achievement, and also in helping teachers overcome racial, ethnic, religious and social class biases that may negatively impact teaching and learning. Effective teachers do not accept failure on the part of their students, and they accept responsibility when their students fail to learn. They do not blame parents, resources, or other factors beyond their control when students fail to learn (Green, 2002). The quality of an urban district's professional development activities often serves as an important benchmark for establishing and lifting consent decrees and other court decisions related to desegregation orders.

Examples of effective professional development activities tailored to urban settings include an initiative at Michigan State University in which former classroom teachers and principals receive up-to-date training so they can go into the classroom and "coach" teachers in urban areas. The Michigan Department of Education is funding this project directed by Dr. Barbara Markle at Michigan State University. A second example is the training received by teachers in the Detroit Public Schools in reading and math, and in Open Court, a specialized reading program developed by McGraw-Hill that has been implemented district-wide. In both of these examples, research-validated strategies in teacher professional development have been utilized to meet the needs of urban schools.

COMMUNITY AND PARENTAL INVOLVEMENT

Community and parental involvement are synonymous with effective schools. A strong and supportive educational environment is provided in communities concerned with effective educational strategies. The direct participation of parents and others in the educational process can represent an irreplaceable resource to schools and school systems. Seeking out and maintaining strong levels of parental and community involvement has come to be thought of as one of the most important goals for a school. Research has shown consistently that high levels of student performance are significantly influenced by levels of parental involvement and general community support. Studies of school effectiveness conducted by Rutter (2002), Marzano (2003), and Bracey (2001), among others, all concluded that parental and community involvement were among the most important influences upon the achievement levels of low income students (see also Ballen & Moles, 1994; Comer & Haynes, 1991; Epstein, 1985, 1995; Henderson & Berla, 1994; Davies, 1994; Bloom, 1992; Green, 1998a).

While parental involvement and community support are known to be important for all students, a critical challenge is to cultivate it among student and parent populations who need it the most—including poor and minority student constituencies in urban environments. In a recent meta-analysis of 20 studies on parental involvement in minority communities, for example, Jeynes (2002) concluded that parental involvement significantly influenced minority students' academic performance across all racial groups included in the study (see also Carr & Wilson, 1997; Carr, 1995; Taylor & Wang, 1997; Dornbusch, Ritter, & Steinberg, 1991). Whereas parental involvement exerts a measurably positive influence upon student academic performance, significant barriers often exist within schools which inhibit the realization of this goal (Baiz Khan, 1996; Liontos, 1991; Lutz & Merz, 1992). These include the fact that the "language" of schools is often not understood by low income and minority parents; teachers and administrators may be resentful of parents intruding upon their authority; and parents who are too willing to cede authority for educating their children to school professionals (Liontos, 1991; Lareau, 1987).

HIGH EXPECTATIONS FOR STUDENT AND TEACHER PERFORMANCE

A final characteristic of effective schools, which is the focus of the remaining discussion of this paper, involves high expectations for student and teacher performance. Stated most directly, high expectations—especially when accompanied by the other characteristics of effective schools summarized earlier—have been shown to play a critical role in determining the academic success of students. Moreover, high expectations are quite logically most important for students—such as the disproportionately poor and non-white children in urban schools—of whom little has been historically expected, and little has too often resulted. My own years of work in urban school systems around the country (see, for example, Green, 2002, 2003) has shown that effective schools operate in, and establish for themselves, a self-sustaining climate in which the professional staff begins with the sincere belief that all students *can* achieve, hold high expectations for student accomplishments, and do whatever it takes to ensure that their students *will* learn.

The following discussion elaborates upon the role played by expectations within our intra-personal and interpersonal lives, along with the critical role they play within our system of education.

EXPECTATIONS: A DRIVING FORCE IN HUMAN BEHAVIOR AND HEALTH

Research in both classical psychology and educational psychology has long shown that the expectations that others have for us—especially those who act as important influences in our lives—affect the way in which we view ourselves. The way we view ourselves, in turn, affects our own expectations for ourselves. Finally, the expectations we hold for ourselves impact our performance, and as a result influence the nature and the quality of the lives we live.

The importance of expectations in a wide array of life experiences has been documented in numerous studies within the field of psychology over the years. Buckley *et al.* (1998) and Thompson and Seiss (1978), for example, demonstrated that job satisfaction is related not only to objective factors, but also to the similarities and differences between our *expectations* for the job and our *perceptions* of it. Shepperd & McNulty (2002) found that when people have advance expectations about how something will turn out, they tend to feel either better about an outcome that exceeds expectations and worse about an outcome that falls short of expectations than would be the case if they had not had expectations at all prior to the event.

Schizophrenics were found to be likely to behave normally if they think the people with whom they are interacting are unaware of their condition (Kreiger & Levin, 1976). Rosenthal & Rubin (1978) identified 345 studies assessing what they called "interpersonal expectancy effects," or the power of peoples' expectations to influence the behavior of others, and concluded that the effects of expectations are very real. Psychological therapists who expect their clients to improve have been found to be more likely to actually have clients who improve (Martin, Moore, & Stern, 1977). Survey respondents interviewed by telephone provide fewer answers when their interviewers expect the questions will be difficult to answer compared to when the interviewers expect the questions will be easy (Singer, Frankel, & Glassman, 1983).

Expectations also seem to operate on the *physical* as well as the *psychological* level, and can have a substantial impact upon health and well-being. Meyer *et al.* (2002), for example, showed that patients' expectancies of treatment effectiveness predicted actual clinical improvement in their condition, suggesting that patients who expect treatment to be effective tend to engage more constructively in session, which helps bring about symptom reduction.

McComas and Moore (2001) observed that high school biology students who were asked to examine the effects of three solutions (labeled as stimulant, depressant, or unknown, but that actually contained only spring water) on their heart rate were quite willing to report effects (heart rate increasing after exposure to stimulant and decreasing after exposure to depressant), despite the fact that such outcomes were physiologically impossible. The perceived taste of some foods and beverages may differ according to their color (Zellner & Durlach, 2003). If we expect a food to taste sweet and it instead tastes bitter, we may experience it as tasting more bitter than it otherwise would (Carlsmith & Aronson, 1963).

The literature on psychosomatic illness (cf. Pelletier, 1976) is replete with studies that show the power of expectations to *improve* as well as to *undermine* physical health. In one experiment (Agras, Horn, & Taylor, 1982), subjects' expectations affected the rate at which their blood pressure fell following periods of relaxation. In another example, mental patients who expect to recover are more likely to actually recover (Block *et al.*, 1976; Cartwright and Cartwright, 1958; Bergman, 1958). Dieters who expect to lose weight are more likely to do so than those who do not expect to lose weight (Foster *et al.*, 1997; Bradley, Poser, & Johnson, 1980). A final well-known example is the increase in the condition *anorexia nervosa*; Hoek & Hoeken (2003), Harrison (2003), Garner, Garfinkel, Schwartz, & Thompson (1980), and other researchers have speculated that this is largely due to changing cultural expectations that many people (primarily adolescent girls and young women) interpret as requiring them to be thin in order to appear attractive.

EXPECTATIONS AND AGENTS OF SOCIALIZATION

Expectations also act as a powerful force in the socialization process, particularly with children. Child psychology literature indicates that most children behave in a certain way much of the time because they are *expected* to behave in accordance with the norms of their culture and environment. As Brophy (1977) has pointed out, it seems that relatively little social and personal development is communicated genetically from one generation to the next. Rather, it appears that children are socialized by means of peer and adult expectations for them, and the treatment (in the form of either rewards or sanctions) that arises from their behavior.

Parents are typically the first important socializing influence in the lives of children, and a substantial body of research indicates that parental expectations have a marked impact on the values, behavior, and goals their children will come to have. Numerous studies on delinquency and antisocial behavior, from serious crime to bullying, have shown that those who commit these kinds of transgressions were likely to have "learned" such behaviors from parents (see Snyder *et al.*, 2003; Espelage, 2003). Parental expectations for their children's behavior, as well as their actions, are also manifested in a wide array of children's behaviors and outcomes ranging from their job aspirations (see Liben *et al.*, 2001) and attitudes toward marriage (see Boyer-Pennington *et al.*, 2001) to their likelihood of eating well and exercising regularly (see Tomson *et al.*, 2003).

Unfortunately, it is well known that parents are by no means the only agent exerting a socializing influence upon children in the form of expectations for their behavior. As Vandell (2000) and Brophy (1977), among others, have pointed out, it is typical for children to be exposed to a vast array of socializing influences—including peers, siblings, the media, and other sources of popular culture—that are in some circumstances even more powerful than parents and may encourage unhealthy and negative behavior. Research by Harris (1995), Vandell (2000) and other psychologists, in fact, has shown that the influence of peers is for many children an even more powerful socializing agent than parents. The authors speculate that this is in part due to the amount of time children spend with peers. Time spent with peers is often far greater than time spent with family, particularly in single parent families in which the parent works long hours or multiple jobs.

It is also increasingly clear that visual media are an all-important agent of socialization in the lives of children today and establishes powerful expectations for their behavior. This is due both to the power of the visual image (Huesman *et al.*, 2003; Wilson *et al.*, 2003; Kellner, 1995; Gitlin, 1986; Lopiano-Misdom & DeLuca, 1997) and the fact that many children spend long periods of time unsupervised in front of televisions and computer screens. Results of a 1998 study of television viewing habits recently reported by the Family and Consumer Sciences Department at Oklahoma State University, for example, notes that the majority of American children watch nearly 20 hours of TV each week, compared to 38 minutes weekly that parents spend talking to their children; this research also notes that the average child spends more than 1500 hours annually watching TV (compared to only 900 in school), and that watching more than 10 hours a week has been shown to exert a negative impact upon academic performance (Oklahoma State University, 2004). Not only has time spent watching television increased, but the violent and sexual content of what is being watched has unquestionably increased. Huesman *et al.* (2003) concluded that there is a link between TV-violence viewing at ages 6 to 10 and adult aggressive behavior about 15 years later. Childhood exposure to media violence predicts young adult aggressive behavior for both males and females. Identification with aggressive TV characters and perceived realism of TV violence also predict later aggression. These relations persist even when the effects of socioeconomic status, intellectual ability, and a variety of parenting factors are controlled, the authors conclude.

Children also learn about societal expectations in the areas of sexuality, relationships, race, and academic achievement through socializing agents such as television and movies, and it is again unfortunate that the "lessons" are often not positive. Even children as young as 18 months begin watching cartoons on television. Thompson and Zerbinos (1992) interviewed children ages 4-9 to learn how cartoons might color the children's view of the world towards much less stereotypical gender portrayal, particularly in female characters. Both boys and girls described boy characters' behavior as violent and active. Children identified very few "real job" behaviors for either boy or girl characters. Thompson and Zerbinos (1995) also content analyzed cartoons and found that male characters were given more prominence, and appeared and talked more frequently than female cartoon characters. This was particularly true in cartoons produced prior to 1980, but which are still aired.

Children watching television, movies, and even news programs are exposed to repeated portrayals of irresponsible sexual behavior and dysfunctional relationships between men and women, and these images often have negative long-lasting impacts as children grow up and begin formulating their own relationships. Television characters who pursue high levels of academic achievement are typically ridiculed and unpopular. While progress has clearly been made with respect to racial stereotyping in popular culture and mass media, old habits and stereotypes often die hard, and children are still far more likely to see non-white characters on TV and in movies as performers, sports stars, and criminals than in roles such as doctors, lawyers, and teachers (see, for example, Buselle & Crandall, 2002; Larson, 2003; Nathanson *et al.*, 2002; Henderson & Baldasty, 2002).

RESEARCH DOCUMENTING
THE IMPORTANCE OF EXPECTATIONS IN EDUCATION

The preceding research and discussion demonstrates the significance of expectations upon human behavior and upon the socialization of children. Given that many children spend more time in school than they do with parents, how, specifically, do expectations function within the educational system, and what impact have expectations been shown to have upon school-related outcomes?

Since at least the 1960s, researchers have found that expectations on the part of teachers and other school staff are a significant determinant of academic outcomes. In one of the most famous experiments in this area, Iowa schoolteacher Jane Elliott (reported in Tozer, Violas, & Senese, 1993) showed in her famous "blue eyes/brown eyes" experiment how readily children could be led to model a teacher's behavior and expectations. Elliott told her third grade class one day that children with blue eyes were inferior to those with brown eyes, and the children quickly replicated her expectations in their treatment of classmates. When she told the class the next day that just the opposite was true (that *brown-eyed* people were inferior), the class readily modeled this expectation too.

Another well-known experiment that tested the effects of teachers' expectations on children's achievement was a study conducted in the mid-1960s by Robert Rosenthal and Lenore Jacobson (1968). They convinced teachers in an elementary school that a test had identified certain students as academic "bloomers." Teachers were told that these bloomers would exhibit a positive spurt in school performance during the upcoming year. The identified children had, in fact, been chosen at random, but after a year's instruction by teachers who expected superior performance, something remarkable happened: students who had been expected to "bloom" did in fact do so. On average, the "bloomers" gained 12 points on an IQ test, compared with 8 points for others. The effect

was greatest for the younger children, with bloomers in the first and second grades gaining a full 14 points, compared with only 4 points for children whose teachers had developed no particularly strong expectations for them.

Numerous other studies conducted around the time of Elliott's and Rosenthal & Jacobson's research in the 1960s and 1970s confirmed their findings, in that high expectations from teachers greatly influence children's academic achievement, even when home factors are held constant. Cahan (1966), McDill *et al.* (1976), Beez (1968), Tuckman & Bierman (1971), Dusek (1975), Brophy & Everston (1976), Brookover & Lezotte (1977), Crano & Mellon (1976), Smead (1981), and Rutter (1982), among others, all found that teachers who *expect* more from their students *get* more. A related finding of significance was that it does not seem to matter whether expectations are artificially induced, as in Elliot and Rosenthal & Jacobson's work, or are formed naturally. One study (Palardy, 1969) showed that teachers who personally believed that boys are less able than girls to read well ended up with boy students who read less well than their girl students. Meanwhile, the students of teachers who believed that boys and girls can read equally well tended to read equally well.

Additional studies showed that the effects of expectations were not confined to elementary schools and young children. In one experiment, for example, Air Force recruits in a mathematics program were randomly split into several classes; their instructors were told that students in some classes were brighter than students in others. Those students whose instructors believed they were teaching brighter classes learned more, on average, than their equally intelligent counterparts of whom less was expected (Shrank, 1968; Martinek, 1980).

More recent research has continued to confirm the importance of expectations in education, for students in general as well as for specific student subgroups. Nauta and Epperson (2003), for example, found that personal expectations among high school girls for careers in science, math, and engineering (which were developed with significant input from teachers, counselors, and other school staff) were an excellent predictor of college majors and aspirations for future leadership roles in these fields. Stone and Lane (2003) found that teacher expectations for student performance were one factor that explained a significant amount of variability in performance among Maryland students on state standardized exams using growth models. Jordan and Stanovich (2001) report that teachers of students with special needs who attribute learning difficulties to permanent characteristics of the student tend to hold lower expectations for the achievement levels of these students, and interacted less frequently with these students than did their teaching colleagues who did not hold such beliefs. On a more anecdotal level, a high school English teacher (Gutchewsky, 2001) reflects on how she successfully used more accurate and unbiased expectations to change the attitude of her reluctant readers toward reading.

EXPECTATIONS AND URBAN STUDENT POPULATIONS

As a larger body of research on effective schools and expectations has emerged, a common theme is that low expectations are especially problematic in urban schools which enroll large numbers of poor and non-white children. As I have stated in earlier work (see Green, 1977, 1996, 2002) urban children are all too often subjected to school influences that erode their self-confidence, whereby teachers expect low performance and children "live down" to these expectations in a self-fulfilling prophecy. Achievement gap data presented previously illustrate the result of this process; other research has helped us understand how it works.

Much of the research on expectations and urban students has focused, quite appropriately, on African American students, and males in particular. In studying the issue of expectations extensively, Harvard University scholar Ronald Ferguson (1998, 2003) concluded that despite the incomplete nature of the research, the evidence suggests that teachers' perceptions, expectations, and behaviors probably do help to sustain, and perhaps even to expand, the test score gap between white and African American students. Swanson *et al.* (2003) examined African American males' perceptions of teacher expectations for their achievement and found that achievement was indeed influenced by negative stereotyping and tracking, as were coping strategies used by the students in school. Davis (2003) identifies several influential theories that explain the poor performance of African American males, including resistance and cultural opposition to schooling and achievement, the social organization of schools (particularly curriculum issues, teaching strategies, school achievement climate, and expectations), and issues of masculine identity, centering on the idea that African American males perceive schooling activities as feminine and irrelevant to their masculine sense of self. Ogbu (1986, 1999, 2003), Fordham (1988), and Fordham and Ogbu (1986) have also studied school expectations for African American students extensively, and suggest that low expectations on the part of teachers contribute to the formation of "oppositional identities" among African American students. In this type of identity, school success is equated with "acting white," and is thus rejected.

Other research has focused on expectations and other minority groups. In studying the impact of expectations upon Latino students, for example, Armandariz (2001) concluded that negative biases toward Mexican Americans are institutionalized in the public school system. Most schools enforce the norms, values, and behaviors of the dominant group; have low teacher expectations for Mexican American students; and systematically devalue the skills, knowledge, and self-concepts learned by Mexican American students in their homes and communities. These factors have an adverse effect on the formation of students' identities, he argues, and many of these children develop "Anglicized" mannerisms as a way of coping within the dominant group processes. In another study involving pre-service teachers' expectations for schools with students of color and second-language learners, Terrill & Mark

(2000) found that participants held significantly different expectations for Native American students in rural schools (as well as for African American students in urban schools) in comparison with from those held for white students in suburban schools. Terrill and Mark also found that participants felt lower levels of comfort and safety when making home visits among Native American and African American students.

Educational researchers and psychologists have documented one of the most common ways in which urban and non-white students are the victims of low expectations, in that they are frequently "tracked" into lower-level class where they are made to feel less intelligent than their majority-group peers. Stanford psychologist Claude M. Steele (1995, 1997, 1998) refers to this phenomenon as "stereotype vulnerability." Stereotypes, Steele argues, affect intellectual test performance. Although all students experience anxiety over possible academic failure, members of disadvantaged groups experience more difficulty because of stereotypical ideas about how well they can and will do academically. They perceive that they are not expected to do well and, thus, do not do well.

Findings of this nature are particularly disturbing because urban and minority children are most in need of high, rather than low, expectations on the part of their teachers in order to counteract the negative environmental influences (poverty, crime, etc.) that many face on a daily basis. They must also struggle to overcome the "curse of low expectations," in which poor and minority children consistently learn from their environment that school success is neither possible nor desirable (see, for example, Hill, 1998; Weinstein, Madison, & Kuklinski, 1995; Kozol, 1967, 1991; Kotlowitz, 1991; MacLeod, 1987; Green, 1977, 1996, 1998a). MacLeod (1987), Brophy & Good (1970), Jussim & Fleming (1996) and others have documented the extent to which this "curse of low expectations" can result in what Merton (1948) first referred to as "self-fulfilling prophecies," in which students for whom low expectations have been held often wind up confirming this judgment. When students constantly see, hear, and experience from their teachers that they are unable to attain high levels of success, they internalize these beliefs and "live down" to the low expectation levels set for them.

Kozol (1991) has also argued that the expectations of poor and minority students in urban schools are often a function of the substandard facilities they attend, as they equate crumbling buildings, leaking roofs and unkempt toilets and floors with the low expectations that the larger society has for them. This same finding has also emerged from my own work in Detroit with Griffore and Phenice, where student achievement—as well as teachers' perceptions of job satisfaction and the ability levels of their students—appear to be correlated with the physical condition of school facilities (Green, 2002; Lippmann, Burns, & MacArthur, 1996; Wang & Gordon, 1994; Taylor, 1994). However, the environment need not drive the education experience in these schools (Green, 1998a).

WHAT ARE TEACHER EXPECTATIONS AND HOW ARE THEY FORMED?

Having established the significance of expectations for school-related outcomes, both in a general sense and specifically for urban student populations, it is useful to turn to how this concept has been defined. Brophy & Good (1990, 1974), who have conducted numerous studies of teacher expectations and their impact, define teacher expectations as "inferences that teachers make about the present and future academic achievement and general classroom behavior of their students." In a general sense, expectations include teachers' beliefs regarding the changeability or fixed nature of their students' abilities, potential on the part of students to benefit from instruction, the level of difficulty that is appropriate for a class or subgroup, and whether the class should be taught as a group or in some smaller subgroup. Teacher expectations for individual students are formed from a number of sources, both real and imagined, including formal or informal student records (test scores, past grades, teacher comments, etc.), knowledge about a student's family, or actual interaction with the student in a classroom setting.

What factors help to determine how expectations are formed? Research indicates that teachers form elaborate sets of expectations for students as early as the third day of school (Ferguson, 1998, 2003; Brophy & Good, 1990; Willis, 1972), and use a wide variety of criteria to formulate these expectations. These criteria, some of which are well-known and have been studied extensively as well as others which are less obvious, can include:

- **Race:** This is among the most-studied area within the literature on expectations. Numerous scholars have documented the tendencies of teachers to set low expectations for their students based on racial/ethnic background (see Ferguson, 1998, 2003; Swanson *et al.*, 2003; Davis, 2003; Haycock, 2001; Barton, 2003; Van Matre *et al.*, 2000; Fordham & Ogbu, 1986; Hale-Benson, 1986; Ross & Jackson, 1991; Rigsby, Stull, & Morse-Kelly, 1997; Chaikin & Derlega, 1978; Adams, 1978).
- **Gender:** Numerous studies have investigated the relationship between expectations and gender, with ample evidence indicating that teachers often hold different expectations for boys and girls by overall expected performance as well as by subject area (see Nauta & Epperson, 2003; Van Matre *et al.*, 2000; Tozer, Violas, & Senese, 1993; Geis, 1993; Fennema *et al.*, 1990; Schlosser & Algozzine, 1980; Adams, 1978).
- **Social class:** Among the more pervasive beliefs shown to influence the formation and persistence of expectations is that poor children cannot or will not learn because they are poor (see Barton, 1993; Davis, 2003; Feller, 2003; Kozol, 1991; Lareau, 1987; Berger, Cohen, & Zelditch, 1972; Brook, Whiteman, Lukoff, & Gordon, 1979; Cooper, Baron, & Lowe, 1975).
- **Disability status:** A substantial number of studies have suggested that lower expectations are often held for students with disabilities ranging from autism and attention deficit

hyperactivity disorder (ADHD) to learning disabilities. Low expectations for these students, in turn, are one explanation for the academic difficulties that students with disabilities often experience (see Cook, 2002; Jordan & Stanovich, 2001; Clark & Artiles, 2000; Milich, McAnnich, & Harris, 1992; Harris *et al.*, 1992; Foster, Schmidt, & Sabatino, 1976; Gillung & Rucker, 1977).

- **Limited English Proficiency (LEP) and English as a Second Language (ESL) status:** LEP and ESL students have been shown to be subjected to lower expectations on the part of their teachers than are native English speakers (see Shin, 2002; Huss-Keeler, 1997; Bermudez, 1994).

- **Student history:** Teachers may use a variety of characteristics related to the educational history of students—including the curricular "tracks" they were in, their behavioral records and psychological reports, previous grades, teacher experiences with siblings of the student, and written reports in student files, to formulate both accurate and inaccurate expectations for their performance (see Farkas, 2003; Macrae, Stangor, & Hewstone, 1996; Jussim & Fleming, 1996; Berends, 1995; Carr & Kurtz-Costes, 1994; Oakes, 1992; Oakes & Lipton, 1992; Urdan, Midgley, & Wood, 1995; Tuckman & Bierman, 1971; MacLeod, 1987; Humphreys & Stubbs, 1977; Adams & Cohen, 1976; Lavoie & Adams, 1974; Mason, 1973; Seaver, 1973).

- **Physical attractiveness:** Youth perceived to be more physically attractive—a concept often intertwined with race and social class—may receive more attention than those perceived as being less attractive (see Eagly *et al.*, 1991; Feingold, 1992; Brophy & Good, 1974).

- **Handwriting and apprehension about writing:** In much the same way as students enter school with differing levels of ability to read, their ability to write—and to do so neatly—varies in accordance with factors such as parental level of education. In turn, teachers can quickly form expectations of students based upon the quality of their writing (see Rosenblum *et al.*, 2003; Hughes, Keeling, & Tuck, 1983; Daly, 1979).

- **Communication and speech patterns:** The ability of students to communicate in linguistic patterns that meet the approval of their teachers and the dominant society has been shown to influence the expectations that teachers develop, as well as the academic success or failure of students (see Farkas, 2003; Ogbu, 1999, 2003; McCroskey & Daly, 1976; Bernstein, 1973, 1975).

- **Participation in extracurricular activities:** Research has indicated that teachers may hold higher academic expectations of students who participated in extracurricular activities compared to students who either did nothing after school or were employed after school (see Van Matre *et al.*, 2000).

WHY AND HOW DO EXPECTATIONS MATTER?

Why would the fact that a teacher expects some students to do better than others result in actual differences in performance? Research has attempted to address this issue by showing not just that expectations influence student achievement, but *how* classroom interaction patterns bring about this relationship. The literature indicates that teacher expectations affect student achievement primarily in two ways: *first,* teachers teach more material more effectively and enthusiastically to students for whom they have high expectations; and *second,* teachers respond more favorably to students for whom high expectations are held—in a host of often subtle ways that seem to boost students' expectations for themselves.

Regarding the amount of material introduced to students and the effectiveness and enthusiasm with which it is taught, early research by Beez (1968) found that Head Start tutors who had been induced to form differential expectations for groups of children introduced nearly twice as much new material to the children they expected to be particularly bright. Despite much similarity in the actual abilities of the children, those for whom the tutors had high expectations learned twice as much as their counterparts for whom low expectations were held. In a later study, Beez (1970) also found

that students for whom teachers had low expectations were given fewer opportunities to learn new material than their high-expectations classmates. More recently, Brimijoin *et al.* (2003) have demonstrated how maintaining data on student achievement can help guide the amount of material introduced to students, and to tailor content to student ability levels. Fiske (1992) has speculated that teachers may unwittingly hold lower expectations for some students and introduce fewer concepts to them because they are forced to "teach to the middle" in classrooms with widely differing ability levels. Children whose actual or perceived abilities are low, therefore, are neglected (as are the brightest pupils) as teachers work mostly with the majority who fall in the middle of the ability range.

In a study involving direct classroom observations, Brophy and Good (1970) found that teachers worked harder to elicit good performances from children for whom they had high expectations, while tending to accept poor performances from children for whom they had low expectations. Some teachers chose students for whom they held high expectations to respond more often to classroom discussions (Good, 1968, 1970; Davis & Levine, 1970;

Rubovitz & Maehr, 1971), and tended to give them more time to formulate answers once they had been chosen (Rowe, 1974; Kester & Letchworth, 1972).

"High expectations" students are also often favored in a host of other ways within the teacher-student interaction. Such students are praised more often and more appropriately than are low expectations students, with the latter being praised less for correct answers and criticized more for incorrect answers (Brimijoin *et al.*, 2003; Witty & DeBaryshe, 1994; Medinnus & Unruh, 1971; Rubovitz & Maehr, 1971; Brophy & Good, 1974). Teachers also exhibit more positive non-verbal behavior toward their high expectations students. One experiment (Chaiken, Sigler, & Derlega, 1972) involved a tutorial situation in which tutors were told that students were of either above average, average, or below average intelligence. Tutors working with children for whom they had high expectations smiled three times more often, nodded up and down two and a half times more often, and looked students in the eye significantly more often. Also, they leaned forward toward high expectations students eight times longer than toward low expectations students. Teachers seem to be generally more encouraging, accepting, and interactive with students for whom they held high expectations (Witty & DeBaryshe, 1994; Martinek & Johnson, 1970).

Research has also shown that the impact of low expectations is frequently seen in how students view themselves in terms of their own ability to succeed, and to relate and adapt to the educational environment. Brookover *et al.* (1979) and Beady (1975), for example, determined that a sense of "academic futility"—in which students perceive their own educational outcomes—was typical of students for whom low expectations had been held, and that this phenomenon accounted for more than half of the variation found among students' academic achievement. Furthermore, they found that teachers' expectations were directly related to students' sense of academic futility. Students who have teachers who expect them to be successful tend to believe they are the "masters" of their own academic fates—and as a result, they tend to work harder and to become more involved in class than do students whose teachers expect little of them. Similarly, exposure to low expectations is also thought to result in students' underestimating their own abilities, and in decreased self-confidence in their capacity to do work they are capable of doing. Students whose classroom experiences reflect low expectations tend to become more discouraged and withdrawn or apathetic. Their achievement levels suffer, and in the long run so do their lives (Tiedeman & Faber, 1995; Faber, 1992; Stipek & Gralinski, 1991; Fry, 1982; Vollmer, 1976; Bandura, 1977).

Perhaps the key point regarding teacher expectations is that formation of such perceptions is normal and inherently neither good nor bad. Expectation formation, in fact, appears to be a very natural process, as studies have shown that even infants form expectations for when they will be fed and the likelihood that their parents will respond to crying (see, for example, Mast, Fagen, & Rovee-Collier, 1980). The critical issue regarding expectations appears to be their *accuracy* and the *flexibility* with which they are held. Expectations become damaging if based upon inaccurate or inflexible information, and if instructional decisions are based upon these incorrect perceptions (Brophy & Good, 1990; Babad, Bernieri, & Rosenthal, 1991; Demaray & Elliott, 1998). Brophy and Good suggest that accurate and flexible expectations can benefit both teacher and student, provided they are continually adjusted to keep in step with the student's actual progress and needs.

In contrast, problems arise when teachers are inaccurate in their perceptions, or when they are too rigid in their evaluations. Bognar (1982) found that many teachers do not revise their expectations of students in response to new information. Cooper (1979) determined that expectations formed prior to observing students affected teacher evaluations even after direct exposure provided additional and presumably more reliable information. The matter is made more serious due to the tendency for people to generalize from expectations formed in one context to expectations in unrelated areas (Berger & Fisek, 1974). Rosenthal and Jacobson (1968), for example, found that teachers evaluated the fictitious "bloomers" not only as academically superior but also as more likely to succeed, more interesting, happier, and more intellectually curious. The point is that expectations should be based upon reasonably accurate information, be flexible, and continually increased to challenge students to achieve to their complete potential.

IMPLICATIONS OF EXPECTATIONS FOR TEACHERS

The primary implication of the preceding discussion for teachers is that if they establish high, accurate, and flexible expectations for all their students, they are likely to function as more effective educators by creating an environment in which high achievement is the norm. Teachers must become increasingly aware of the ways in which their expectations affect classroom behavior, and they must modify this behavior, where appropriate, in order to teach all students effectively. In terms of helping teachers develop specific strategies for reaching this ideal, Brophy and Good (1974, 1990) identified three types of teachers:

- **Proactive** teachers are those that establish and maintain the initiative in structuring interactions with their classes as groups, as well as with individual students. Their expectations for students are used in the planning of activities designed to individualize students and maximize their achievement, but expectations are generally accurate and kept flexible. One model for how one teacher has used assessment data to differentiate instruction so that each student is appropriately challenged is presented by Brimijoin *et al.,* (2003).

- **Reactive,** or passive, teachers adjust their actions to students according to students' behavior, and allow students to control or condition the patterns of teacher-student interaction in the classroom.

- **Overactive** teachers not only allow themselves to be conditioned by student differences, but exacerbate these differences by treating the students as even more different than they really are. It is this type of teacher who will be more prone to favor students who show good performance and/or desirable classroom behavior, and to reject or to give up easily on students who show poor performance and/or undesirable classroom behavior.

Teachers who desire to be effective, of course, should strive to adopt the premises and behaviors of the proactive, rather than the reactive or overactive teacher. Brophy and Good (1974) are generally optimistic about their ability to do so, as they indicate that

much teacher behavior is unconscious. If one assumes that this factor, and not callousness, indifference, or irresponsibility is the major cause of

inappropriate classroom teaching, it follows that much inappropriate
teaching can be eliminated simply by making teachers more aware of what
they are doing (p. 277).

Lezotte *et al.* (1980) add that virtually every type of classroom activity presents an opportunity for teachers to communicate expectations to students. Because teachers may not be aware of how their expectations manifest themselves and are perceived by students, they suggest that a three-step process be undertaken:

- **First,** teachers should evaluate as honestly as possible the intended expectations they have communicated or will communicate to students. They should communicate clear, specific, and ambitious standards for their classes, and teach difficult material in several different ways if necessary. Professional development activities, in addition to regular teacher evaluations by peers and principals, may provide an ideal means of accomplishing this task.
- **Second,** teachers might consider asking students themselves how they (the teachers) convey expectations regarding performance and behavior. Are high expectations just rhetoric, or are they institutionalized in daily activities and monitored regularly? This might best be accomplished by means of an anonymous questionnaire, perhaps accompanied by semi-structured interviews, role-playing simulations, and interactions with parents in settings such as parent-teacher conferences.
- **Finally,** teachers may wish to team with colleagues to observe themselves in instruction. A colleague may be in a good position to note what signals are being conveyed to students, and why messages sent by teachers may differ from those perceived by students.

SUMMARY

A great deal of research on teaching and effective schools over the past several decades has reached the same general conclusion: all children can learn if provided with a context conducive for doing so. It is similarly clear that a significant piece of this context is high expectations on the part of teachers and all school staff for the achievement of students. Teachers can help all students reach high levels of achievement if they hold high expectations and put in place within their classrooms the practices and supports that turn high expectations into achievement and success. This is the central conclusion of the author, and is one that should be the foundation of efforts on the part of every district, school, principal, and teacher in planning for the future.

High expectations are particularly important in creating more effective urban schools, whose students have become disproportionately poor and non-white, and have suffered for years from the "curse of low expectations." Research has clearly and consistently shown that while teacher expectations exert a measurable effect upon the academic performance of all students, they are particularly important for poor and non-white children who grow up in urban environments stricken by poverty, crime, family dysfunction, and other social maladies. For years, these problems were  offered as excuses for poor performance and low levels of achievement in urban schools, but recent research on effective schools, as well as legislative changes that increase the accountability of schools to students and parents, has demonstrated that high levels of poverty need not, and should not, doom all urban students to failure and a life of hardship.

My own work, as well as a good deal of research on teacher effectiveness, provides examples of settings in which high expectations are a key component in "beating the odds" in urban schools. Dallas and Detroit offer good examples of urban districts I have worked with in which high expectations have been institutionalized into all aspects of the educational process, and their efforts are being replicated in districts and schools across the country. These efforts have been rewarded with improved levels of student achievement and a renewed sense of optimism that better days are ahead. Scholars who continue to research the most effective educational practices are another piece of the solution, as they develop and publicize ways of ensuring that high expectations can become a reality, rather than simply an empty slogan.

Given the well-documented relationship shown to exist between success in education and in life, both on an individual as well as a societal level, bringing the goal of high expectations and high achievement into classrooms across America must continue to be a priority of the highest order. It is important to note that expectations alone are not enough to bring about high achievement; they must instead be coupled with effective instructional practices and other characteristics of effective schools if the desired results are to be obtained. Research clearly shows, however, that genuinely high expectations are a necessary starting point in bringing about high achievement for all students. Our nation as a whole will be better off when high expectations for student success are widely held by teachers and school administrators, and all children benefit from this belief by reflecting higher levels of academic achievement.

"No other intervention can make the difference that a knowledgeable, skillful teacher can make in the learning process."

"Doing What Matters Most," 1997

EXPECT𝘈𝘵IONS

How Teacher Expectations Can Increase
Student Achievement and Assist in
Closing the Achievement Gap

Section II

What Effective Teachers Do:
Best Practices

WHAT RESEARCH SAYS EFFECTIVE TEACHERS DO

With a growing realization of just how true those words are, preparing and sustaining effective teachers in the classrooms of America's schools is becoming a priority of the highest order in educational policy, especially in schools with significant numbers of poor and racial minority students. As both past and present research confirms the difference that properly trained teachers using the most effective techniques can make in the educational experiences of our children, the movement to cultivate effective teaching—a major component which is related to the expectations teachers hold for their students—is growing.

This section reviews and summarizes important findings from research on effective teaching and best practices, focusing on the all-important role of high expectations in the educational process. It provides examples of what teachers can do to make high expectations work in the classroom for all students and thereby increase student achievement. In attempting to increase the academic achievement of low income students and racial minority students, teachers are looking for strategies. This document is an effort to suggest from the literature and from years of university teaching, administration, and observation and consulting what teachers can do to increase student achievement. The purpose is to help teachers in classrooms in which children may not be as fully prepared academically as students who come from wealthier homes. As Fischer *et al.* (1996) note, "The answer to the question of who ends up where is that people's social environments largely influence what rung of the ladder they end up on" (p. 8). They also note:

> "The amount of schooling young Americans receive heavily determines the jobs they get and the income they make. In turn, educational policies—what sorts of schools are provided, the way school resources are distributed (usually according to the community in which children live), teaching methods such as tracking, and so on—strongly affect how much schooling children receive (p. 9).

It is important, therefore, not to underestimate what teachers can do to improve the educational experience for all youngsters, particularly racial minorities and those who come from disadvantaged backgrounds. A resourceful, skillful and committed teacher can make a tremendous difference in the acquisition of knowledge (Darling-Hammond, 1997). We must do all we can to assist teachers to grow and develop in a continuing way in order that they can become effective instructional leaders in their classrooms with high expectations for student success.

CHARACTERISTICS, PRACTICES, AND SKILLS OF THE MOST EFFECTIVE TEACHERS

1. Effective teachers maintain an overall atmosphere (verbal and non-verbal) of general encouragement and support for the learning process of all students—and not just specific to student responses to teacher questioning. They generate a supportive, positive, and challenging atmosphere in the classroom. They act as a major resource of information and support to students.

The most important factor in allowing all students to perform to their maximum ability is a conviction on the part of the teacher in the ability of students to learn. Effective teachers sincerely believe that all students can and *will* learn in their classrooms, and teachers, using proper motivational and instructional strategies, can and *will* teach all students in their classroom. Everything they do conveys this positive approach to students that they *will* learn in this class.

2. Effective teachers maintain an orderly environment that is safe, structured, and comfortable. They should create a sense that this is a place to concentrate on the learning at hand, rather than on immediate anxieties and distracting events in the school, home or neighborhood environment.

Effective teachers maintain an orderly environment that facilitates learning without being rigid or dictatorial. By being inclusive, they give their students a sense that they have a stake in the "community." As part of that community, they accept responsibility for taking care of classroom (and school) resources and participating in school activities. The norm of positive student behavior develops when discipline procedures are perceived to be fair and that they apply equally to all. Teachers must model the kind of behavior they wish students to display. Positive rewards and praise are the major techniques used to create desired behavior. When undesired behavior by students occurs, humiliation and violence are never used. Punitive and authoritarian attitudes are not demonstrated. Discipline is handled in the classroom itself wherever possible and not referred outside. Preferably, it is handled, at least in part, by students themselves. "Firm but fair" behavior is expected, and a clear definition of standards is conveyed at the start of the term and communicated to all students.

3. Effective teachers not only have high expectations but also set clear standards of attainable academic and behavioral performance, and hold students to them.

Students must know precisely *what* is expected of them and *why* it is expected, and believe they can meet those expectations. As much as possible, they should be empowered and have played a part in setting those standards. Students should see standards upheld, and know

40

specific consequences related to each standard. Standards should be consistent and equally applied to all students, but teachers are reasonable in enforcement when conditions become modified. Good behavior should receive positive reinforcement.

4. Effective teachers carefully think, plan, and make decisions to ensure strategic teaching.

Teachers need to plan for appropriate instruction time, for smooth transitions during the academic period, and for pacing of instruction to enhance the use of instructional time. Teachers need to create the appropriate atmosphere and the conditions that create strategic learning. New learning must be linked to prior learning; it must connect application of current information and skills into new situations; it must be organized; and it must be goal-driven. This takes a great deal of time and foresight.

5. Effective teachers call on *all* students to participate in classroom discussions with challenging questions, in multiple forms, related to the cognitive information being covered. Effective teachers appreciate the importance of every student.

All students can and should participate in class activities. Frequently, certain students tend to monopolize attention because they have had past success and develop confidence in their ability to ask questions and respond with quality answers. *All* students should be helped to develop this sense of success and confidence. Care must be given to structure activities so that all students succeed, and, over time, develop skills in class discussion and other activities. All students have imagination and capability for thinking. Effective teachers see their role as "consultants" who help to guide students.

6. Effective teachers give students adequate time to formulate answers when called upon. "Wait time" is used to cultivate good responses.

One strategy that is frequently used is the "Wait-Listen-Wait" technique. Students need time to develop their answers, and often, by being provided with extra time, will reach answers on their own. Effective teachers allow complete and extended silence. Giving students more time—even those who may think they are done—will cause them to add more and develop their own thoughts more fully. Teachers should also listen fully to what students say. Students may not use the same words as the teacher would choose, but they are, nevertheless, equally valid. Teachers should let students' answers go where they will, then wait to see if other students have listened. (This helps to honor student responses and gives all of them confidence to contribute). When the student has finished, instead of answering, effective teachers ask other students to react. If more input is needed, the teacher helps the students to formulate their own responses through skillfully shaped questions. Teacher leadership can be demonstrated by cultivating a student's response.

7. Effective teachers help to lead students into correct answers, using encouragement and clues, and by developing and shaping answers interactively—probe, restate questions, give hints, etc.; reinforce good responses in multiple ways.

Research indicates that some teachers allow "better" students more time to answer, and also help them to reach their answers through shaping. The most effective teachers do this for *all* students. This allows students to develop academic mastery, critical thinking skills, and self-esteem based on success. They honor student responses and help them to shape and expand upon their responses through leading questions and "wait-listen-wait." Then, they ask other students what additional points might be added. Generally, effective teachers do not answer any question which a student can answer for him/herself.

8. Effective teachers structure opportunities for students to achieve significant success:
- **assure cognitive entry attained;**
- **task breakdown;**
- **ordered sequencing;**
- **mastery learning model: presentation, guided practice, independent practice, review, assessment, re-instruction, and reinforcement.**

While there is some variation in the ways that mastery learning techniques are implemented, its basic strategies for permitting students to succeed are accepted. Students need the *will* and the *skill* to learn; the mastery learning paradigm provides this. Students who learn and then have the opportunity to practice what they have learned will retain the most. Research indicates this is a major indicator of effective teaching. Students who feel successful academically, personally, and socially develop self-worth and the willingness to make efforts to achieve in school.

9. Effective teachers react to student responses with praise:
- **appropriate in time and quantity; directed and specific;**
- **not general, stereotyped, and/or single-worded.**

All teachers give pupils reinforcement and praise, but research indicates that there are sharp differences in the type of praise given. "Low expectations" teachers praise less for correct answers and criticize more for incorrect answers. "High expectations" teachers praise correct answers more *often* and more *appropriately,* and shape incorrect answers into correct ones that can be praised. All students need praise, but they are quick to identify insincere, "phony" praise. They need genuine, appropriate, and specific praise that provide cues as to what they need to pursue and develop.

10. Effective teachers use significant amounts of positive <u>non-verbal behavior as well</u>:
- **<u>smile;</u>**
- **<u>nod positively;</u>**
- **look students directly in the eye;**
- **<u>lean forward;</u>**
- **encourage more than one direct response.**

Non-verbal behavior, as a part of the teacher's overall reward system, is the most immediate to the teacher and can be one of the most subtly motivating or discouraging forces available to teachers in their interaction with students. It is almost always noticed by students, especially when others are receiving it, and is often unperceived by the teacher using it. One classic study found that tutors who were told that students they were teaching were talented, acted in the following ways: they smiled three times more often, nodded up and down two-and-a-half times more often, and leaned forward eight  times more often. As with praise (described above), the stimulus becomes self-fulfilling and brings the expected response. Effective teachers are keenly aware of their ability to influence behavior through non-verbal mechanisms and use them adeptly.

11. Effective teachers <u>design learning activities</u> to be <u>challenging</u>, engaging, relevant, and <u>directed to student motivations</u>; emphasize the process of learning and its excitement as a quest.

Students will <u>no longer accept material that is not engaging or relevant</u>. They can find relevance in a system, however, that shows purpose. Learning is an <u>ongoing</u> process and <u>teachers must prepare students for lifelong participation</u>. Some questions have no right answers, and some of today's right answers will shift in coming years. Students must be prepared for change. Emphasizing that learning is a *process* also permits teachers to admit their own fallibility and, because students feel less threatened, they are more motivated to participate.

12. Effective teachers are proactively available; actively assist students and demonstrate willingness to help both during class and non-class time; encourage students who are "response-reticent."

Students who feel alienated in their personal or academic lives frequently need an adult "significant other" who can provide guidance and direction, and can assume the tremendous responsibility of being someone who cares about their life. Young people need responsible role models who can inspire students to follow in their ways. Effective teachers holistically integrate their approach to students, seeing students as total persons and allowing them to be seen in the same way. Good teachers are intensely human and *have,* as well as *show,* positive feelings.

13. Effective teachers give adequate evaluative feedback and constructive criticism that are, and are perceived as, positive and instructional.

Effective teachers measure students' progress frequently and share those results with students in a timely, directed, and productive way. Since students respond with greater or lesser validity to different measurement methods, different types of assessment should be used. Teachers should not use feedback as a predictor of student failure, but as a method for diagnosis of additional knowledge needed, different teaching strategies that should be employed, and stage of readiness for further effort. Teachers need to show students that measurement of their progress is a continuing, non-threatening process and is not intended to become a mechanism for failure. One way to do this is to include students in the assessment process and to ask for their input and comments. Another is to show students how evaluation is helpful to them. Evaluation needs to be accompanied by plans for what to do with the results—plans that are constructive and positive.

14. Effective teachers place primary stress on academic role definition, and do not settle for solely social or other non-academic goals.

While social relations are important to students, and flexibility on the part of the teacher is necessary, there must be a focus on the primary role of the school and the classroom as educational entities. Settling for "social adjustment" results when teachers do not accept that all students can and will learn, and that this is their primary responsibility. When other objectives are pursued, they should be primarily to facilitate maximization of the overall goals of education. It is through academic success that students will gain in self-worth and feelings of high expectation for their own achievement. Teachers must set expectations for high quality work based on the students' level of ability. Effective evaluation should determine what reasonable and attainable levels of performance are warranted. Students should be rewarded, in a structured fashion, for trying to meet and then exceeding the levels which they have helped to identify and establish.

15. Effective teachers appreciate and celebrate diversity in the classroom.

A quick demographic comparison of the students in our nation's schools with the composition of its teaching force suggests an emerging "diversity gap" that must be addressed, if all students are to reach their full potential (Orfield & Lee, 2004). In addition to school districts seeking out higher numbers of qualified minority teachers and teacher training institutions doing more to attract minority candidates (both of which are largely beyond the control of individual teachers), current teachers must continually familiarize themselves with the diverse set of talents and issues brought into classrooms by different groups of students. This must come from enhanced teacher training and from continued professional development activities, of course, but it must also come from individual teachers who make a committed effort at *becoming* and *remaining* informed about and aware of issues related to diversity in the classroom. This is especially true in cities with multiple diverse groups such as San Francisco and Dallas as well as uniracial districts such as Detroit and Atlanta. Diversity should be celebrated in those communities and teachers should be sensitive to it not only in multiracial urban districts but also in school districts that are white, suburban, segregated and racially isolated. Students should be introduced to concepts of diversity so they will be more open-minded in their attitudes about other races and cultures.

16. Effective teachers continually update their skills.

It has become increasingly clear that a "crisis of qualifications" has emerged within too many American schools. One recent study indicated that more than one-fourth of newly hired teachers nationwide lacked the qualifications for their job, and almost the same proportion (23%) of all secondary teachers lacks even a minor in their main teaching field. This crisis is particularly acute in urban schools serving high-poverty and predominantly minority students, where this same study found (among other things) that urban students had less than a 50% chance of getting a math or science teacher who was both licensed and had a degree in his/her field.

Rectifying this grim situation, of course, is largely the task of federal and state governments, teacher training institutions, and school districts, which must place a higher priority on teacher training and credentialing. It is also the prerogative of individual teachers, however, who must (for the good of their students) pursue and continually update their training and skills, in order that they are familiar with the latest and most effective teaching techniques. There are some districts that are outstanding in selecting and motivating highly trained and properly credentialed teachers. In Detroit more than 63% of classroom teachers have master's degrees or higher.

17. Effective teachers participate in induction, mentoring, and collaborative activities with experienced teachers.

Current research on teaching has also pointed to a strong relationship between effective teachers and those who participated in mentoring, induction activities, and collaboration and observation of experienced "master teachers" within their district and building. As is the case with diversity training and the updating of teachers' skills, this is an area that will require broad, system-level change (such as a reevaluation of what qualities and skills teachers should have, and a devoting of the time and resources to obtain them) that is largely beyond the ability of individual teachers to change by themselves. It is also the case, however, that teachers must make conscientious and continued efforts to avail themselves of the expertise of their experienced colleagues, whose experience has been shown to be critical in the development of effective teachers.

SELECTED BIBLIOGRAPHY

Adams, G.R. (1978). "Racial Membership and Physical Attractiveness Effects on Pre-School Teachers' Expectations." *Child Studies Journal* 8 (1), 29-41.

Adams, G.R. and A.S. Cohen. (1976). "Characteristics of Children and Teacher Expectancy Extension to Child's Social and Family Life." *Journal of Educational Research* 70 (2), 87-90.

Agras, W.S., M. Horne, and C.B. Taylor. (1982). "Expectations and the Blood Pressure Lowering Effects of Relaxation." *Psychosomatic Medicine* 44 (4), 389-395.

Anyon, J. (1997). *Ghetto Schooling: A Political Economy of Urban Educational Reform.* New York: Teachers College Press.

Armendariz, A.L. (2001). "The impact of racial prejudice on the socialization of Mexican American students in the public schools." *Equity & Excellence in Education* 33(3), 59-63.

Association for Supervision and Curriculum Development. (1990). *Update* 32.

Austin, B.W. (ed.) (1996). *Repairing the Breach: Key Ways to Support Family Life, Reclaim Our Streets, and Rebuild Civil Society in America's Communities.* Dillon, Colo.: Alpine Guild, Inc.

Babad, E., F. Bernieri, and R. Rosenthal. (1991). "Students as Judges of Teachers' Verbal and Non-Verbal Behavior." *American Educational Research Journal* 28 (1), 211-234.

Baiz Kahn, M. (1996). "Parental Involvement in Education: Possibilities and Limitations." *School Community Journal* 6 (1), 57-68.

Ballen, J. and O. Moles. (1994). *Strong Families, Strong Schools: Building Community Partnerships for Learning.* Washington, D.C.: U.S. Department of Education.

Bandura, A. (1977). "Self-Efficacy: Toward a Unifying Theory of Behavioral Change." *Psychology Review* 81, 191-215.

Banks, J.A. (ed.) (1995). *Handbook of Research on Multicultural Education.* New York: Macmillan.

Bartell, C.A. (1995). "Shaping Teacher Induction Policy in California." *Teacher Education Quarterly* 22 (4), 27-44.

Barton, P. (2003). *Parsing the Achievement Gap: Baselines for Tracking Progress.* Princeton, New Jersey: Educational Testing Service.

Beady, C.H. (1975). "Systemic Interpretation of an Analysis of the Relationship Between Academic Climate Variables and Achievement in Predominantly Black Elementary Schools." Unpublished doctoral dissertation, Michigan State University.

Beez, W.V. (1968). "Influence on Biased Psychological Reports of Teacher Behavior and Pupil Performance." Proceedings of the 76th annual convention of the American Psychological Association 3, 605-606.

Beez, W.V. (1970). "Influence in Biased Psychological Reports on Teacher Behavior and Pupil Performance." In M.W. Miles and W.W. Charters, Jr. (eds.), *Learning in School Settings.* Boston: Allyn and Bacon.

Benjamin, R. (1979). "Toward Effective Urban Schools: A National Study." In D. Brundage (ed.), *Journalism Research Fellows Report: What Makes an Effective School?* Washington, D.C.: George Washington University.

Berends, M. (1995). "Educational Stratification and Students' Social Bonding to School." *British Journal of the Sociology of Education* 16, 327-351.

Berger, J., B.P. Cohen, and M. Selditch. (1972). "Status Characteristics and Social Interaction." *American Sociological Review* 37, 241-255.

Bergman, P. (1958)."The Role of Faith in Psychotherapy." *Bulletin of the Menninger Clinic* 22, 92-103.

Berliner, D.C. and B.J. Biddle (1995). *The Manufactured Crisis: Myths, Fraud, and the Attack on America's Public Schools.* Reading: Addison-Wesley.

Bermudez, A. (1994). *Doing Our Homework: How Schools Can Engage Hispanic Communities.* Charleston, West Virginia: Appalachian Educational Laboratories, Inc.

Bernstein, B.B. (ed.). (1973). *Class, Codes, and Control: Applied Studies Toward a Sociology of Language (Vol. 2).* London, Boston: Routledge and Kegan Paul.

Bernstein, B.B. (ed.). (1975). *Class, Codes, and Control: Toward a Theory of Educational Transmissions (Vol. 3).* London: Routledge and Kegan Paul.

Biddle, B.J. and D.C. Berliner. (2002). "Small Class Size and its Effects." *Educational Leadership* 59(5), 12-23.

Block, J.H. (ed.). (1971). *Schools, Society, and Mastery Learning.* New York: Holt, Rinehart, and Winston.

Block, J.H. (ed.). (1974). *Mastery Learning: Theory and Practice.* New York: Holt, Rinehart, and Winston.

Block, S., F. Bond, B. Qualls, I. Yalom, and E. Zimmerman. (1976). "Patients' Expectations of Therapeutic Improvement and Their Outcomes." *American Journal of Psychiatry* 133 (12), 1457-1460.

Bloom, J. (1992). *Parenting Our Schools: A Hands-On Guide to Educational Reform.* Toronto: Little, Brown, and Co.

Bognar, C.J. (1982). "Dissonant Feedback about Achievement and Teachers' Expectations." *Alberta Journal of Education* 28 (3), 277-287.

Boocock, S.P. (1972). *An Introduction to the Sociology of Learning.* Boston: Houghton-Mifflin Co.

Boutte, G.S. (1992, June). "Frustrations of an African-American Parent: A Personal and Professional Account." *Phi Delta Kappan* 6, 786-788.

Boyer-Pennington, M.E., J. Pennington, and C. Spink. (2001). "Students' expectations and optimism toward marriage as a function of parental divorce." *Journal of Divorce & Remarriage* 34 (3/4), 71-87.

Bracey, G.W. (2001). "School Involvement and the Working Poor." *Phi Delta Kappan* 82 (10), 795.

Bradley, I., E.G. Poser, and J.A. Johnson. (1980). "Outcome Expectation Ratings as Predictions of Success in Weight Reduction." *Journal of Clinical Psychology* 36 (2), 500-502.

Brimijoin, K. Marquissee, E., and C.A. Tomlinson. (2003). "Using Data to Differentiate Instruction." *Educational Leadership* 60 (5), 70-73.

Brook, J.S., M. Whiteman, I.F. Lukoff, and A.S. Gordon. (1979). "Maternal and Adolescent Expectations and Aspirations as Related to Sex, Ethnicity, and Socioeconomic Status." *Journal of Genetic Psychology* 135 (2), 209-216.

Brookover, W., C., Beady, P. Flood, J. Schweitzer, and L. Wisenbaker. (1979). *School Social Systems and Student Achievement: Schools Can Make a Difference*. South Hadley: J.F. Bergon Co. (distributed by Praeger Publishers, New York).

Brookover, W. and L. Lezotte. (1977). *Changes in School Characteristics Coincident with Changes in Student Achievement*. East Lansing: Michigan State University College of Urban Development.

Brophy, J.E. (1977). *Child Development and Socialization*. Chicago: Scientific Research Associates.

Brophy, J. and C. Everston. (1976). *Learning from Teaching: A Developmental Perspective*. Boston: Allyn and Bacon.

Brophy, J. and T. Good. (1970). "Teachers' Communication of Differential Expectations for Childrens' Classroom Performance: Some Behavioral Data." *Journal of Educational Psychology* 61, 365-374.

Brophy, J.E. and T.L. Good. (1974). *Teacher-Student Relationships: Causes and Consequences*. New York: Holt, Rinehart, and Winston.

Brophy, J. (ed.) (1998). *Advances in Research on Teaching. Volume 7: Expectations in the Classroom*. Greenwich, Conn.: JAI Press.

Buckley, M.R., D.B. Fedor, and J.G. Veres. (1998). "Investigating newcomer expectations and job-related outcomes." *Journal of Applied Psychology* 83 (3), 452-461.

Bunzel, John H. (ed.). (1985). *Challenge to American Schools: The Case for Standards and Values*. New York: Oxford University Press.

Busselle, R. and H. Crandall. (2002). "Television Viewing and Perceptions About Race Differences in Socioeconomic Success." *Journal of Broadcasting & Electronic Media* 46(2), 265-282.

Cahan, L.S. (1966). "Experimental Manipulation of Bias in Teachers' Scoring of Subjective Tests." Paper presented at the American Psychological Association, New York.

Carano, W.D. and P.M. Mellon. (1978). "Casual Influence of Teachers' Expectancies on Children's Academic Performance: A Cross-Lagged Panel Analysis." *Journal of Educational Psychology* 70 (1), 39-49.

Carlsmith, J.M. and E. Aronson. (1963). "Some Hedonic Consequences of the Confirmation and Disconfirmation of Expectancies." *Journal of Abnormal and Social Psychology* 66, 151-156.

Carr, A. (1995). "Race, Class, and Gender Differences in School Change Team Membership." *Race, Gender, and Class* 3 (1), 79-96.

Carr, A.A. and R. Wilson. (1997). "A Model of Parental Participation: A Secondary Data Analysis." *School Community Journal* 7 (2), 9-24.

Carr, M. and B.E. Kurtz-Coates. (1994). "Is Being Smart Everything? The Influence of Student Achievement on Teachers' Perceptions." *British Journal of Educational Psychology* 64, 263-276.

Carroll, J.B. and J.S. Chall (eds.). (1975) *Toward a Literate Society: A Report from the National Academy of Education.* New York: McGraw-Hill.

Carroll, J.S. (1978). "Effect of Imagining an Event on Expectations for the Event." *Journal of Experimental Social Psychology* 14 (1), 88-96.

Cartwright, D. and R. Cartwright. (1958). "Faith and Improvement in Psychotherapy." *Journal of Experimental Social Psychology* 5, 174-177.

Chaiken, A.L. and V.J. Derlega. (1978). "Nonverbal Mediators of Expectancy Effects in Black and White Children." *Journal of Applied Social Psychology* 8 (2), 117-125.

Chaiken, A., E. Sigler, and V. Derlega. (1972). "Nonverbal Mediators of Teacher Expectancy Effects." Unpublished manuscript, Old Dominion University.

Chinn, C.A., M.A. Waggoner, R.C. Anderson, M. Schommer, and I.A. Wilkinson. (1993). "Situated Actions During Reading Lessons: A Microanalysis of Oral Reading Error Episodes. *American Educational Research Journal* 30 (2) (Summer), 361-392.

Clark, M.D. and A.J. Artiles. (2000). "A cross-national study of teachers' attributional patterns: A study of elementary schools in California and Guatemala City." *The Journal of Special Education* 34(2), 77-89.

Coleman, J. *et al.* (1966). "Equality of Educational Opportunity." Washington: U.S. Department of Health, Education, and Welfare.

Comer, J.P. (1995). *School Power: Implications of an Intervention Project.* New York: Free Press.

Comer, J.P. (ed.). (1996). *Rallying the Whole Village: The Comer Process for Reforming Education.* New York: Teachers College Press.

Comer, J.P. (1997). *Waiting for a Miracle: Why Schools Can't Solve Our Problems—And How We Can.* New York: Dutton.

Comer, J. and N. Haynes. (1991). "Parent Involvement in Schools: An Ecological Approach." *Elementary School Journal* 91, 271-277.

Conway, D. and R.R. Verdugo. (1999). "Fear-free education zones: creating safe schools in New Jersey." *Education and Urban Society* 31 (3), 357-367.

Cook, B.G. (2002). "Inclusive Attitudes, Strengths, and Weaknesses of Pre-service General Educators Enrolled in a Curriculum Infusion Teacher Preparation Program." *Teacher Education and Special Education* 25 (3), 262-277.

Cooper, H.M. (1979). "Some Effects of Performance Information on Academic Expectations." *Journal of Educational Psychology* 71 (3), 373-380.

Cotton, Kathleen. (2003). *Principals and Student Achievement.* Alexandria, Virginia: Association for Supervision and Curriculum Development.

Council of the Great City Schools. (2001). *Beating the Odds: A City-By-City Analysis of Student Performance and Achievement Gaps On State Assessments.* Washington, D.C.: Author.

Council of the Great City Schools. (2002). *Beating the Odds II: A City-By-City Analysis of Student Performance and Achievement Gaps On State Assessments.* Washington, D.C.: Author.

Council of the Great City Schools. (2003a). Big-City Schools Post Significant Gains in 4th Grade Reading On Nation's Report Card. Available at http://www.cgcs.org/pressrelease/2003/12-17-03.html, January 23, 2004.

Council of the Great City Schools. (2003b). *Beating the Odds III: A City-By-City Analysis of Student Performance and Achievement Gaps On State Assessments.* Washington, D.C.: Author.

Daly, J.A. (1979). "Writing Apprehension in the Classroom—Teacher Role Expectancies of the Apprehensive Writer." *Research in the Teaching of English* 13 (1), 37-44.

Danielson, C. (2001). "New Trends in Teacher Evaluation." *Educational Leadership* 58 (5), 12-15.

Darling-Hammond, L. (1997). *The Right to Learn: A Blueprint for Creating Schools That Work.* San Francisco: Jossey-Bass.

Darling-Hammond, L. (2001). "The Challenge of Staffing Our Schools." *Educational Leadership* 58 (8), 12-17.

Darling-Hammond, L., A.E. Wise, and S. Klein. (1994). *A License to Teach: Building a Profession for 21st Century Schools.* Boulder: Westview Press.

Darling-Hammond, L. and P. Youngs. (2002). "Defining 'Highly Qualified Teachers': What Does 'Scientifically-Based Research' Actually Tell Us?" *Educational Researcher* 31 (9), 13-25.

Davies, D. (1994, October 12). "Partnerships for Reform." *Education Week.*

Davis, D. and G. Levine. (1970). "The Behavioral Manifestations of Teachers' Expectations." Unpublished manuscript, Hebrew University of Jerusalem.

Davis, J.E. (2003). "Early Schooling and Academic Achievement of African American Males." *Urban Education* 38 (5), 515-537.

Demaray, M.K. and S. N. Elliott. (1998). "Teachers' Judgments of Students' Academic Functioning: A Comparison of Actual and Predicted Performances." *School Psychology Quarterly* 13 (1), 8-24.

Desimone, L., M. Garet, and B. Birman. (2003). "Improving Teachers' In-Service Professional Development in Mathematics and Science: The Role of Postsecondary Institutions." *Educational Policy* 17 (5), 613-649.

Dornbusch, S.M., P.L. Ritter, and L. Steinberg. (1991). "Community Influences on the Relation of Family Statuses to Adolescent School Performance: An Attempt to Understand a Difference Between African Americans and non-Hispanic Whites. *American Journal of Education* 99, 543-567.

Douglas, J.W. (1964). *The Home and School: A Study of the Ability and Attainment in the Primary School.* London: MacGibbon and Kee.

Dusek, J.B. (1975). "Do Teachers Bias Children's Learning?" *Review of Educational Research* 45, 661-684.

Eagly, A.H., R.D. Ashmore, M.G. Makhijani, and L.C. Longo. (1991). "What is Beautiful is Good, but . . . : A Meta-Analysis of Research on the Physical Attractiveness Stereotype." *Psychological Bulletin* 110, 109-128.

Edmonds, R. (1979). "Effective Schools for the Urban Poor." *Educational Leadership,* 37: 15-24.

Entwisle, D.R. and M. Webster. (1978). "Raising Expectations Indirectly." *Social Forces* 57 (1), 257-264.

Education Week on the Web (2004, Jan. 14). Education Issues A-Z: No Child Left Behind. Available at http://www.edweek.com/context/topics/issuespage.cfm?id=59.

Epstein, J. (1985). "Home and School Connections in Schools of the Future: Implications of Research on Parent Involvement." *Peabody Journal of Education* (Planning the School of the Future) 62, 18-41.

Epstein, J. (1995). "School/Family/Community Partnerships: Caring for the Children We Share." *Phi Delta Kappan*, May, 701-713.

Espelage, D.L., Holt, M.K., and Henkel, R.R. (2003). "Examination of Peer-Group Contextual Effects on Aggression During Early Adolescence." *Child Development* 74 (1), 205-220.

Evans, J.F. (2002). "Effective Teachers: An Investigation from the Perspectives of Elementary School Students." *Action in Teacher Education* 24 (3), 51-62.

Faber, G. (1992). "Fourth Graders' Spelling-Specific Self-Perceptions: An Empirical Analysis of Their Relationship to Self-Concept and Achievement. *Zeitschrift fur Padagogische Psychologie* 6, 185-196.

Farkas, G. (2003). "Racial Disparities and Discrimination in Education: What Do We Know, How Do We Know It, and What Do We Need to Know?" *Teachers College Record* 105 (6), 1119-1146.

Feingold, A. (1992). "Good-Looking People are Not What We Think." *Psychological Bulletin* 111, 304-341.

Feller, B. (2003). Urban scores below national average, but other comparisons show promise. Available at http://www.canarsiecourier.com/News/2003/0626/OtherNews/024.html.

Fennema, E., P. Peterson, T.R. Carpenter, and C.A. Lubinski.(1990). "Teachers' Attributions and Beliefs About Girls, Boys, and Mathematics." *Educational Studies in Mathematics* 21, 55-69.

Ferguson, R.F. and H.F. Ladd. (1996). "How and Why Money Matters: An Analysis of Alabama Schools." In H. Ladd (ed.), *Holding Schools Accountable*. Washington: Brookings Institution, 265-298.

Fermanich, M. (2002). "School Spending for Professional Development: A Cross-Case Analysis of Seven Schools in One Urban District." *Elementary School Journal* 103 (1), 27-50.

Ferguson, R.F. (2003). "Teachers' Perceptions and Expectations and the Black-White Test Score Gap." *Urban Education* 38 (4), 460-507.

Ferguson, R.F. (1998). "Teacher Perceptions and Expectations and the Black-White Test Score Gap." In C. Jenks and M. Phillips (Ed.), *The Black-White Test Score Gap.* Washington, D.C.: The Brookings Institution Press.

Fine, J. and R.C. Cienkus. (1997). "Teacher Effectiveness: The Ultimate Educational Reform Issue." *The High School Journal* 80, 215-294.

Finn, J.D. (2002). "Small classes in American schools: research, practice, and politics." *Phi Delta Kappan* 83(7), 551-560.

Fiske, E.B. (1992). *Smart Schools, Smart Kids: Why Do Some Schools Work?* New York: Touchstone.

Fischer, C.S., M. Hout, M.S.Jankowski, S.R. Lucas, A. Swidler, and K. Voss. (1996). *Inequality by Design: Cracking the Bell Curve Myth.* Princeton, N.J.: Princeton University Press.

Foster, G.D., T.A. Wadden, and R.A. Vogt. (1997). "What is a reasonable weight loss? Patients' expectations and evaluations of obesity treatment outcomes." *Journal of Consulting and Clinical Psychology* 65, 79-85.

Foster, G.G., M.S. Schmidt, and D. Sabatino. (1976). "Teacher Expectancies and the Label 'Learning Disabilities.'" *Journal of Learning Disabilities* 9 (2), 111-114.

Fry, P.S. (1982). "Pupil Performance Under Varying Teacher Conditions of High and Low Expectations and High and Low Controls." *Canadian Journal of Behavioral Science* 14 (3), 219-231.

Fuchs, L.S., D. Fuchs, K. Karns, C.L. Hamlett, S. Dutka, and M. Katzarof. (1996). "The Relationship Between Student Ability and the Quality and Effectiveness of Explanations. *American Educational Research Journal* 33 (3) (Fall), 234-258.

Fullan, M. (2002). "Leadership and Sustainability." *Principal Leadership (Middle School Education)* 3 (4), 14-17.

Ganser, T. and M.A. Wham. (1998). "Voices of Cooperating Teachers: Professional Contributions and Personal Satisfaction. *Teacher Education Quarterly* 25 (2) (Spring), 43-52.

Garner, D.M., P.E. Garfinkel, D. Schwartz, and M. Thompson (1980). "Cultural Expectations of Thinness in Women." *Psychology Report* 47 (2), 483-491.

Geis, F.L. (1993). "Self-Fulfilling Prophecies: A Social Psychological View of Gender." In A. Ball and R. Steinberg (eds.), *The Psychology of Gender.* New York: Guilford, 1993.

Gigliotti, R.J. and W. Brookover. (1975). "The Learning Environment: A Comparison of High and Low Achieving Elementary Schools." *Urban Education* 10, 245-261.

Gillung, T.B. and C.N. Rucker. (1977). "Labels and Teacher Expectations." *Educational Children* 43 (7), 464-465.

Gitlin, T. (1986). *Watching Television: A Pantheon Guide to Popular Culture.* New York: Pantheon.

Good, T.L. (1968). "Student Achievement Level and Differential Opportunity for Classroom Response. Unpublished doctoral dissertation, Indiana University.

Good, T.L. (1970). "Which Pupils do Teachers Call On?" *Elementary School Journal* 70, 190-198.

Good, T.L. and J.E. Brophy. (1997). *Looking in Classrooms (7th Edition)*. New York: Longman.

Grant, G. (1985). "Schools That Make an Impact: Creating a Strong Positive Ethos." In J.H. Bunzel (ed.), *Challenge to American Schools: The Case for Standards and Values*. New York: Oxford University Press, 1985, 127-146.

Green, R.L. (1977). *The Urban Challenge—Poverty and Race*. Chicago: Follett.

Green, R.L. (1985a). "Consultants' Year-End Report: Memphis Effective Schools Project." Report presented to the Memphis City Schools.

Green, R.L. (1985b). "Desegregation." In R.L. Green (ed.) *Metropolitan Desegregation*. Washington: Plenum Press.

Green, R.L. (1987). *Expectations: Research Implications on a Major Dimension of Effective Schooling*. Cleveland: Cuyahoga Community College.

Green, R.L. (1996). "A Profile of African American Males." In B.W. Austin (ed.) *Repairing the Breach*. Dillon, Colo.: Alpine Guild, Inc.

Green, R.L. (1998a). *Ownership, Responsibility and Accountability for Student Achievement*. Dillon, Colo.: Alpine Guild, Inc.

Green, R.L. (1998b). *Ownership, Responsibility and Accountability for Student Achievement: First-Year Progress Report*. San Francisco: San Francisco Unified School District.

Green, R.L. (2002). *An Assessment of Student Achievement in the Dallas Independent School District: Final Report*. East Lansing, Michigan: Author.

Green, R.L. (2003). *Evaluation of School Improvement in the Detroit Public Schools–Phase II Final Report*. East Lansing, Michigan: Urban Affairs Programs, Michigan State University.

Gutchewsky, K. (2001). "An attitude adjustment: how I reached my reluctant readers." *English Journal* 91 (2), 79-85.

Hale-Benson, J. (1986). *Black Children—Their Roots, Culture, and Learning*. Baltimore: Johns Hopkins University Press.

Hallinger, P. and J.R. Murphy (1986). "The Social Context of Effective Schools." *American Journal of Education* (May), 328-355.

Harris, J.R. (1995). "Where is the child's environment? A group socialization theory of development." *Psychological Review* 102, 458-489.

Harris, M.J., R.Milich, E.M. Corbitt, D.W. Hoover, and M. Brady. (1992). "Self-Fulfilling Effects of Stigmatizing Information on Children's Social Interactions." *Journal of Personality and Social Psychology* 63, 41-50.

Harrison, K. (2003). "Television Viewers' Ideal Body Proportions: The Case of the Curvaceously Thin Woman." *Sex Roles* 48 (5/6), 255-264.

Hawley, S.H. and R.C. Hawley (1989). *Teacher's Handbook of Practical Strategies for Teaching Thinking in the Classroom*. Amherst, MA: ERA.

Haycock, K. (2001). "Closing the Achievement Gap." *Educational Leadership* 58 (6), 6-11.

Haycock, K. (2002). "Assessing Student Learning: A Practical Guide." *Teacher Librarian* 29 (5), 39.

Henderson, A.T. and N. Berla. (1994). *A New Generation of Evidence: The Family is Critical to Student Achievement.* Washington, D.C.: National Committee for Citizens in Education.

Henderson, J.J. and G.J. Baldasty. (2002). "Race, Advertising, and Prime-Time Television." *Howard Journal of Communications* 14 (2), 97-112.

Hill, Paul. (1998). *Fixing Urban Schools.* Washington, D.C.: Brookings Institution Press.

Hirsch, E.D., Jr. (1996). *The Schools We Need and Why We Don't Have Them.* New York: Doubleday.

Hoek, W.H. and D. Hoeken. (2003). "Review of the Prevalence and Incidence of Eating Disorders." *International Journal of Eating Disorders* 34 (4), 383-396.

Hoge, J.D., S.J. Foster, and P. Nickell. (2002). "Mandatory School Uniforms: A Debate for Students." *Social Education* 66 (5), 284-291.

Hopkins, D., J. Beresford, and M. West. (1998). "Creating the Conditions for Classroom and Teacher Development." *Teachers and Teaching: Theory and Practice* 4 (1) (March), 115-141.

Howell, F.M. and W. Frese. (1953). "Race, Sex, and Aspirations: Evidence for the 'Race Convergence Hypothesis.'" *Sociology of Education* 33, 186-203.

Howey, K. and N. Zimpher (eds.). (1991) *Restructuring the Education of Teachers: Report of the Commission on the Education of Teachers Into the 21st Century.* Reston, VA: Association of Teacher Educators.

Huesman, L.R., J. Moise-Titus, and C. Podolski. (2003). "Longitudinal Relations Between Children's Exposure to TV Violence and Their Aggressive and Violent Behavior in Young Adulthood: 1977-1992." *Developmental Psychology* 39 (2), 201-221.

Hughes, J.N. (2002). "Authoritative Teaching: Tipping the Balance in Favor of School vs. Peer Effects." *Journal of School Psychology* 40 (6), 485-492.

Hughes, D.C., B. Keeling, and B.F. Tuck. (1983). "Effects of Achievement Expectations and Handwriting Quality on Scoring Essays." *Journal of Educational Measurement* 20 (1), 65-70.

Humphreys, L.G. and J. Stubbs. (1977). "Longitudinal Analysis of Teacher Expectation, Student Expectation, and Student Achievement." *Journal of Educational Measurement* 14 (3), 261-270.

Huss-Keeler, R.L. (1997). "Teacher Perception of Ethnic and Linguistic Minority Parental Involvement and its Relations to Children's Language and Literacy Learning: A Case Study." *Teaching and Teacher Education* 13 (2), 171-182.

Jencks, C. (1992). *Rethinking Social Policy: Race, Poverty, and the Underclass.* Cambridge, Mass.: Harvard University Press.

Jencks, C. and P. Peterson (eds.). (1991). *The Urban Underclass.* Washington, D.C.: Brookings Institution Press.

Jencks, C. and M. Phillips (eds.). (1998). *The Black-White Test Score Gap.* Washington, D.C.: Brookings Institution Press.

Jeynes, W.H. (2003). "A Meta-Analysis: The Effects of Parental Involvement on Minority Children's Academic Achievement." *Education and Urban Society* 35 (2), 202-218.

Johnson, J.P., M. Livingston, and R.A. Schwartz. (2000). "What Makes a Good Elementary School? A Critical Examination." *Journal of Educational Research* 93 (6), 339-348.

Jones, B.F., *et al.* (ed.). (1987). *Strategic Teaching and Learning: Cognitive Instruction in the Content Areas.* Chicago: North Central Regional Educational Laboratory.

Jordan, A. and P.J. Stanovich. (2001). "Patterns of teacher-student interaction in inclusive elementary classrooms and correlates with student self-concept." *International Journal of Disability, Development, and Education* 48 (1), 33-52.

Jussim, L. and C. Fleming (1996). "Self-Fulfilling Prophecies and the Maintenance of Social Stereotypes: The Role of Dyadic Interactions and Social Forces. In Macrae, C.N., C. Stangor and M. Hewstone (eds.) *Stereotypes and Stereotyping*. New York: The Guilford Press, 1996, 161-192.

Jussim, L., A. Smith, S. Maden, and P. Palumbo (1998). "Teacher Expectations." In J. Brophy (ed.) *Advances in Research on Teaching. Volume 7: Expectations in the Classroom.* Greenwich, Conn.: JAI Press, 1998.

Kamens, M.W. (1997). "A Model for Introducing Student Teachers to Collaboration." *The Teacher Educator* 33 (2) (Autumn), 90-102.

Kang, H. (1996). "Helping Teachers Thrive on Diversity and Change." *Teacher Education Quarterly* 23 (4), 75-84.

Keiny, S. (1996). "A Community of Learners: Promoting Teachers to Become Learners." *Teachers and Teaching: Theory and Practice* 2 (2) (October), 243-272.

Kellner, D. (1995). *Media Culture: Cultural Studies, Identity, and Politics Between the Modern and the Postmodern.* New York: Routledge.

Kester, S. and G. Letchworth. (1972). "Communication of Teacher Expectations and Their Effect on Achievement and Attitudes of Secondary School Students." *Journal of Educational Research* 66, 51-55.

King, A. (1994). "Guiding Knowledge Construction in the Classroom: Effects of Teaching Children How to Question and How to Explain." *American Educational Research Journal* 31 (2) (Summer), 338-368.

Kotlowitz, A. (1991). *There Are No Children Here: The Story of Two Boys Growing Up in the Other America.* New York: Doubleday.

Kozol, J. (1968). *Death at an Early Age: The Destruction of the Hearts and Minds of Negro Children in the Boston Public Schools.* Boston: Houghton Mifflin.

Kozol, J. (1991). *Savage Inequalities: Children in America's Schools.* New York: Crown.

Krieger, M.J. and S.W. Levin. (1976). "Schizophrenic Behavior as a Function of Role Expectation." *Journal of Clinical Psychology* 32 (2), 463-467.

Lareau, A. (1987). "Social Class Differences in Family-School Relationships: The Importance of Cultural Capital." *Sociology of Education* 60, 73-85.

Larson, M.S. (2003). "Gender, Race, and Aggression in Television Commercials That Feature Children." *Sex Roles* 48 (1/2), 67-75.

Lavoie, J. and G. Adams. (1974). "Teacher Expectancy and its Relationship to Physical and Interpersonal Characteristics of the Child." *Alberta Journal of Educational Research* 20, 120-132.

Lembo, J.M. (1969). *Psychology of Effective Classroom Instruction*. Cleveland: Charles E. Merrill.

Lezotte, L.W. (1980). *Climate Characteristics in Instructionally Effective Schools*. East Lansing, Michigan: Michigan State University Center for Urban Affairs, College of Urban Development.

Lezotte, L., D.V. Hathaway, S.K. Miller, J. Passalacqua, and W. Brookover. (1980). *School Learning Climate and Student Achievement*. East Lansing: Michigan State University.

Liben, L.S., R.S. Bigler, and H.R. Krogh. (2001). "Pink and blue collar jobs: children's judgments of job status and job aspirations in relation to sex of worker." *Journal of Experimental Child Psychology* 79 (4), 346-363.

Lippmann, L., S. Burns, and E. MacArthur. (1996). *Urban Schools: The Challenge of Location and Poverty* (NCES-184). Washington, D.C.: U.S. Department of Education, National Center for Education Statistics.

Lopiano-Misdom, J. and J. DeLuca. (1997). *Street Trends: How Today's Alternative Youth Cultures are Creating Tomorrow's Mainstream Markets*. New York: HarperCollins.

Lutz, F. and C. Merz. (1992). *The Politics of School/Community Relations*. New York: Teachers College Press.

Macrae, C.N., C. Stangor, and M. Hewstone. (1996). *Stereotypes and Stereotyping*. New York: Guilford Press.

MacLeod, J. (1995). *Ain't No Makin' It: Aspirations and Attainment in a Low Income Neighborhood*. Boulder: Westview Press.

Martin, P.J., J.E. Moore, and A.L. Sterne (1977). "Therapists as Prophets—Their Expectancies and Treatment Outcomes." *Psychotherapy Theory, Research, and Practice* 14 (2), 188-195.

Martinek, T. and S. Johnson. (1976). "Teacher Expectation: Effects of Dydactic Interaction and Self-Concept in Elementary Age Children." *Research Quarterly* 46, 80-86.

Martinek, T.J. (1980). "Students' Expectations as Related to a Teacher's Expectations and Self-Concept in Elementary Age Children." *Perception and Motor Skills* 50 (2), 555-561.

Marzano, R.J. (2003). "Using Data: Two Wrongs and a Right." *Educational Leadership* 60 (5), 56-60.

Mason, E. (1973). "Teachers' Observations and Expectations of Boys and Girls as Influenced by Biased Psychological Reports and Knowledge of the Effects of Bias." *Journal of Educational Psychology* 65, 238-243.

Mast, V.K., J.W. Fagen, and C.K. Rovee-Collier. (1980). "Immediate and Long-Term Memory for Reinforcement Context—The Development of Learned Expectancies in Early Infancy." *Child Development* 61 (3), 700-707.

Mayes, M. (1998, Sept. 1). "Smaller Classes Get Big Praise." *Lansing State Journal*, p. 1B.

McCafferty, D. (1998, Sept. 25-27). "Downsizing the Classroom." *USA Weekend*, pp. 4-5.

McComas, W.F. and L.S. Moore. (2001). "The expectancy effect in secondary school biology laboratory instruction: issues and opportunities." *The American Biology Teacher* 63 (4), 246-252.

McCroskey, J.C. and J.A. Daly (1976). "Teachers' Expectations of the Communication Apprehensive Child in the Elementary School." *Human Communications* 3 (1), 181-189.

McDill, E.L., E.D. Meyers, Jr., and L.C. Rigsby. (1967). "Institutional Effects on the Academic Behavior of High School Students." *Sociology of Education* 40,181-189.

McEvoy, J. & D. Rhodes. (2003). "The Top 10 Mistakes Principals Make." *Principal* 83(1), 20-21.

Means, G., R. Means, J. Castleman, and B. Elsom. (1971). "Verbal Participation as a Function of the Presence of Prior Information Concerning Aptitude." *California Journal of Educational Research* 22, 58-63.

Medinnus, G. and R. Unruh (1971). "Teacher Expectations and Verbal Communications." Paper presented at the annual meeting of the Western Psychological Association.

Merton, R.K. (1948). "The Self-Fulfilling Prophecy." *Antioch Review* 8, 193-210.

Meyer, B., P.A. Pilkonis, and J.L. Krupnick. (2003). "Treatment Expectancies, Patient Alliance, and Outcome: Further Analyses from the National Institute of Mental Health Treatment of Depression Collaborative Research Program." *Journal of Consulting and Clinical Psychology* 70 (4), 1051-1055.

Milich, R., C.B. McAninch, and M.J. Harris. (1992). "Effects of Stigmatizing Information on Children's Peer Relations: Believing is Seeing." *School Psychology Review* 21 (3), 400-409.

Morrison, F.J. and C.M. Connor. (2002). "Understanding Schooling Effects on Early Literacy: A Working Research Strategy." *Journal of School Psychology* 40 (6), 493-500.

Nathanson, A.I., J. McGee, and B.J. Wilson. (2002). "Counteracting the Effects of Female Stereotypes on Television via Active Mediation." *Journal of Communication* 52 (4), 922-937.

National Center for Education Statistics. (2002). Annual Earnings of Young Adults. Available at http://nces.ed.gov/programs/coe/2002/section2/indicator16.asp.

National Center for Education Statistics. (2003). National Assessment of Educational Progress Data. Available at http://nces.ed.gov/nationsreportcard/naepdata.

National Commission on Teaching and America's Future. (1997). *Doing What Matters Most: Investing in Quality Teaching*. New York: Author.

Nauta, M.M. and D.L. Epperson. (2003). "A Longitudinal Examination of the Social-Cognitive Model Applied to High School Girls' Choices of Nontraditional College Majors and Aspirations." *Journal of Counseling Psychology* 50 (4), 448-457.

Network for Effective Schools. (1987). *Expecting the Best: Effective Publication for all Students—A Report of the Findings of a Major School Reform Study*. New York: Kellwynn Press.

Oakes, J. (1992). "Can Tracking Research Inform Practice? Technical, Narrative and Political Considerations. *Educational Researcher* 21, 12-21.

Oakes, J. and M. Lipton. (1992). "Detracking Schools: Early Lessons from the Field." *Phi Delta Kappan* 73, 448-454.

Ogbu, J.U. (2003*). Black American students in an affluent suburb: a study of academic disengagement.* New York: Lawrence Erlbaum.

Ogbu, J.U. (1999). "Beyond language: ebonics, proper English, and identity in a black-American speech community." *American Educational Research Journal* 36 (2), 147-184.

Oklahoma State University, Family and Consumer Sciences. (2004, Jan. 20). Parenting Issues: Television and Viewing Habits. Available at http://fcs.okstate.edu/parenting/issues/tv.htm.

Olmedo, I.A. (1997). "Challenging Old Assumptions: Preparing Teachers for Inner-City Schools. *Teaching and Teacher Education* 13 (3), 245-258.

Orfield, G. (1994). "The Growth of Segregation in American Schools: Changing Patterns of Segregation and Poverty since 1968. *Equity and Excellence in Education* 27 (1), 5-8.

Orfield, G. and S.E. Eaton. (1996). *Dismantling Desegregation: The Quiet Reversal of Brown v. Board of Education.* New York: The New Press.

Orfield, G. and Lee, C. (2004). Brown *at 50: King's Dream or Plessy's Nightmare?* Cambridge, Mass.: Harvard University.

Palardy, J. (1969). "What Teachers Believe—What Children Achieve." *Elementary School Journal* 69, 370-374.

Peaker, G.F. (1967). "The Regression Analysis of the National Survey." In *Children and their Primary Schools: A Report of the Central Advisory Council for Education.* London: H.M.S.O.

Pelletier, K.R. (1976). *Mind as Healer, Mind as Slayer.* New York: Dell Publishing Co.

Perkins-Gough, D. (2002). "Beyond Instructional Leadership." *Educational Leadership* 59 (8), 95-96.

Peterson, P. (1972). "A Review of the Research on Master Learning Strategies." Unpublished manuscript, International Association for the Evaluation of Educational Research and Development in Teaching. Palo Alto, Calif.: Stanford University.

Phillips, J. (2003). "Powerful Learning: Creating Learning Communities in Urban School Reform." *Journal of Curriculum and Supervision* 18 (3), 240-258.

Porter, A., B. Birman, and L. Desimone. (2003). "Discussion of 'What makes professional development effective,' by T. R. Gusky." *Phi Delta Kappan* 85 (3), 249.

Pressley, M., S.E.Dolezal, L.M. Raphael, L. Mohan, A.D. Roehrig, and K. Bogner. (2003). *Motivating Primary-Grade Students.* New York: The Guilford Press.

Rashid, H.M. (2000). "Professional development and the urban educator: strategies for promoting school as community." *Contemporary Education* 71 (2), 56-59.

Redding, S. (1997). "Academic Achievement, Poverty, and the Expectations of Parents and Teacher." *School Community Journal* 7 (2), 87-103.

Reynolds, D. (1998). "Schooling for Literacy: A Review of Research on Teacher Efficacy and School Efficacy and Its Implications for Contemporary Educational Policies." *Educational Review* 50 (2), 147-162.

Rigsby, L.C., J.C. Stull, and N. Morse-Kelley. (1997). "Determinants of Student Educational Expectations and Achievement: Race/Ethnicity and Gender Differences." In R.D. Taylor and M.C. Wang (eds.), *Social and Emotional Adjustment and Family Relations in Ethnic Minority Families*. Mahwah, N.J.: Lawrence Erlbaum Associates.

Robelen, E.W. (2004, Jan. 16). "No Child" Law Faulted in Democratic Race, *Education Week on the Web*. Available at http://www.edweek.com/ew/ewstory.cfm?slug=18dems.h23.

Robinson, G.E. (1985). "Effective Schools Research: A Guide to School Improvement." *Concerns in Education*. Arlington: Educational Research Service.

Rosenblum, S., P.L. Weiss, and S. Parush. (2003). "Product and Process Evaluation of Handwriting Difficulties." *Educational Psychology Review* 15 (1), 41-81.

Rosenthal, R. and L. Jacobson. (1968). *Pygmalion in the Classroom*. New York: Holt, Rinehart, and Winston.

Rosenthal, R. and D.B. Rubin. (1978). "Interpersonal Expectancy Effects—The First 345 Studies." *Behavior and Brain Science* 1 (3), 377-386.

Ross, S.I. and J.M. Jackson. (1991). "Teachers' Expectations for Black Males' and Black Females' Academic Achievement." *Personality and Social Psychology Bulletin* 17 (1), 78-82.

Rowe, M. (1974). "Wait Time and Rewards as Instructional Variables: Their Influence on Language, Logic, and Fate Control." *Journal of Research in Science* II (4), 291-308.

Rubovitz, P.C. and M.L. Maehr. (1971). "Pygmalion Analyzed: Toward an Explanation of the Rosenthal-Jacobson Findings." *Journal of Personal and Social Psychology* 19, 197-203.

Rutter, M., B. Manghan, P. Mortimer, A. Ouston, and A. Smith. (1979). *Fifteen Thousand Hours: Secondary Schools and Their Effects on Children*. Cambridge: Harvard University Press.

Rutter, M., and M. Maughan. (2002). "School Effectiveness Findings 1979-2002." *Journal of School Psychology* 40 (6), 451-475.

Sack, J. (1999). "Class Size, Teacher Quality Take Center Stage at Hearing." *Education Week* 18 (34), 22.

Schempp, P., S. Tan, D. Manross, and M. Fincher. (1998). "Differences in Novice and Competent Teachers' Knowledge. *Teachers and Teaching: Theory and Practice* 4 (1) (March), 9-20.

Schlosser, L. and B. Algozzine (1980). "Sex, Behavior, and Teacher Expectancies." *Journal of Experimental Education* 43 (3), 231-236.

Schrank, W. (1968). "The Labeling Effect of Ability Grouping." *Journal of Educational Research* 68, 51-52.

Seaver, W.B. (1973, December). "Effects of Naturally Induced Teacher Expectancies." *Journal of Personality and Social Psychology*, 333-342.

Sherman, S.J. (1983). "Expectation-Based and Automatic Behavior—A Comment." *Social Psychology Quarterly* 46 (1), 66-70.

Shepperd, J.A. and J.K. McNulty. (2002). "The affective consequences of expected and unexpected outcomes." *Psychological Science* 13 (1), 85-88.

Shin, S.J. (2002). "Understanding ESL writers: second language writing by composition instructors." *Teaching English in the Two-Year College* 30 (1), 68-75.

Singer, E., M.R. Frankel, and M.B. Glassman (1983). "The Effect of Interviewer Characteristics and Expectations on Responses." *Public Opinion Quarterly* 47 (1), 68-83.

Sizer, T.R. (1984). *Horace's School: Redesigning the American High School.* Boston: Houghton-Mifflin.

Sizer, T.R. (1992). *Horace's Compromise: The Dilemma of the American High School.* Boston: Houghton-Mifflin.

Sizer, T.R. (1996). *Horace's Hope: What Works for the American High School.* Boston: Houghton-Mifflin.

Slavin, R.E. (1980). "Cooperative Learning." *Review of Educational Research* 50 (2), 315-342.

Sleeter, C.E. and C.A. Grant. (1993). *Making Choices for Multicultural Education: Five Approaches to Race, Class, and Gender.* New York: Macmillan.

Smead, V.S. and C.I. Chase. (1981). "Student Expectations as they Relate to Achievement in 8th Grade Mathematics." *Journal of Educational Research* 6, 115-120.

Smith, J.B., R.L. Green, and N.J. Hammond. (1987). *Program Evaluation of Operation Jobs for Youth: Governor's Demonstration Projects.* Cleveland: Cuyahoga Community College.

Smith, P., A. Molnar., and J. Zahorik. (2003). "Class-Size Reduction: A Fresh Look at the Data." *Educational Leadership* 61 (1), 72-74.

Snyder, J., M. Brooker, and M.R. Patrick. (2003). "Observed Peer Victimization During Early Elementary School: Continuity, Growth, and Relation to Risk for Child Antisocial and Depressive Behavior." *Child Development* 74 (6), 1881-1898.

Solomon, P.G. (2002). *The Assessment Bridge: Positive Ways to Link Tests to Learning, Standards, and Curriculum Improvement.* New York: Corwin Press.

Squires, D.A., W.G. Huitt, and J.K. Segars. (1983). *Effective Schools and Classrooms: A Research-Based Perspective.* Alexandria: Association of Supervision and Curriculum Development.

Steele, C.M. (1995). "Stereotype Threat and the Intellectual Test Performance of African Americans." *Journal of Personality and Social Psychology* 69 (5): 797.

Steele, C.M. (1997). "A Threat in the Air: How Stereotypes Shape Intellectual Identity and Performance." *The American Psychologist* 52 (6): 613.

Steele, C.M. (1998). "Stereotyping and Its Threat Are Real." *The American Psychologist* 53 (6): 680.

Stipek, D.J. and J.H. Gralinski. (1991). "Gender Differences in Children's Achievement-Related Beliefs and Emotional Responses to Success and Failure in Mathematics." *Journal of Educational Psychology* 83, 361-371.

St. John, N. (1972). "Mothers and Children: Congruence and Optimism of School-Related Attitudes." *Journal of Marriage and the Family* 34, 422-430.

Stone, C.A. and S. Lane. (2003). "Consequences of a State Accountability Program: Examining Relationships between School Performance Gains and Teacher, Student, and School Variables." *Applied Measurement in Education* 16 (1), 1-26.

Swanson, D.P., M. Cunningham, and M.B. Spencer. (2003). "Black Males' Structural Conditions, Achievement Patterns, Normative Needs, and Opportunities." *Urban Education* 38 (5), 608-633.

Taddonio, J.L. (1975). "Attitudes and Expectancies in ESP Scoring." *Journal of Parapsychology* 39, 289-296.

Taylor, R.D. (1994). "Risk and Resilience: Contextual Influences on the Development of African-American Adolescents." In M.C. Wang and E.W. Gordon (eds.), *Educational Resilience in Inner-City America: Challenges and Prospects*. Hillsdale, N.J.: Lawrence Erlbaum Associates, 119-130.

Taylor, R. and M.C. Wang (eds.). (1997). *Social and Emotional Adjustment and Family Relations in Ethnic Minority Families*. Mahwah, N.J.: Lawrence Erlbaum Associates.

Terrill, M.M. and D.L. Mark. (2000). "Preservice teachers' expectations for schools with children of color and second-language learners." *Journal of Teacher Education* 51 (2), 149-155.

Thompson, A.P. and T.F. Seiss (1978). "Subjective Expectation, Outcome, Discrepancy, and Job Satisfaction." *Canadian Journal of Behavioral Science* 10 (3), 248-257.

Tiedemann, J., and G. Faber (1994). "Girls and Mathematics in Elementary School: Results of a Four-Year Longitudinal Study of Gender Differences in Achievement." *Zeitschrift fur Entwicklungspsychologie und Padagogische Psychologie* 26, 101-111.

Thompson, T. and E. Zerbinos. (1992). "Television Cartoons: Do Children Notice It's a Boy's World?" Paper presented at the annual meeting of the Association for Education in Journalism and Mass Communication. ERIC ED376539.

Thompson, T. and E. Zerbinos. (1995). "Gender Roles in Animated Cartoons: Has the Picture Changed in 20 Years?" *Sex Roles: A Journal of Research* 32 (9-10) 651-673.

Tomson, L.M., R.P. Pangrazi, and G. Friedman. (2003). "Childhood Depressive Symptoms, Physical Activity and Health Related Fitness." *Journal of Sport and Exercise Psychology* 25 (4), 419-439.

Tozer, S.E., P.C. Violas, and G. Senese. (1993). *School and Society: Educational Practice as Social Expression*. New York: McGraw-Hill.

Tucker, M.S. and J.B. Codding (1998). *Standards For Our Schools: How to Set Them, Measure Them, and Reach Them*. San Francisco: Jossey-Bass.

Tuckman, B. and M. Bierman. (1983). "Beyond Pygmalion: Galeta in the Schools." Paper presented at the annual meeting of the American Educational Research Association.

Ubben, G.C., L.W. Hughes, and C.J. Norris. (2001). *The Principal: Creative Leadership for Effective Schools (4th Edition)*. Boston: Allyn & Bacon.

Uchiyama, K.P. and S.A. Wolf. (2002). "The Best Way to Lead Them." *Educational Leadership* 59 (8), 80-83.

Urdan, T., C. Midgley, and S. Wood. (1995). "Special Issues in Reforming Middle Level Schools." *Journal of Early Adolescence* 15, 9-37.

Vandel, D.L. (2000). "Parents, peer groups, and other socializing influences." *Developmental Psychology* 36 (6), 699-710.

Vollmer, F. (1976). "Determinants of Expectancy of Examination Results." *Scandinavian Journal of Psychology* 17 (3), 238-245.

Walberg, H.J. (1984). "Families as Partners in Educational Productivity." *Phi Delta Kappan* 65, 397-400.

Wang, M.C. and E.W. Gordon (eds.). (1994). *Educational Resilience in Inner-City America: Challenges and Prospects*. Hillsdale, N.J.: Lawrence Erlbaum Associates.

Wang, M.C., G.D. Haertel, and H.J. Walberg (1995, December 1993/January 1994). "What Helps Students Learn?" *Laboratory for Student Success,* 74-79.

Wehlage, G. (1986). "At-Risk Students and the Need for High School Reform." Presentation at the Council of Great City Schools Summer Seminar (Detroit, Michigan).

Weinstein, R.S., S.M. Madison, and M.R. Kuklinski. (1995). "Raising Expectations in Schooling: Obstacles and Opportunities for Change." *American Educational Research Journal* 32 (1), 121-159.

White, K.A. (2000). "Do School Uniforms Fit?" *School Administrator* 57 (2), 36-40.

Willis, S. (1972). "Formation of Teachers' Expectations of Students' Academic Performance." Unpublished doctoral dissertation, University of Texas-Austin.

Wilson, B.J., S.L. Smith, and W.J. Potter. (2002). "Violence in children's television programming: assessing the risks." *Journal of Communication* 52(1), 5-35.

Wilty, J. and B.D. DeBaryshe. (1994). "Self-Fulfilling Prophecies and the Maintenance of Social Stereotypes: The Role of Dyadic Interactions and Social Forces." In C.N. Macrae, C. Stangor, and M. Hewstone (eds.), *Stereotypes and Stereotyping*. New York: The Guilford Press, 1996, 161-192.

Wood, G.H. (1992). *Schools That Work: America's Most Innovative Public Education Programs*. New York: Dutton.

Zellner, D.A. and P. Durlach. (2003). "Effect of color on expected and experienced refreshment, intensity, and liking of beverages." *The American Journal of Psychology* 116 (4), 633-647.

PHOTO CREDITS